Band Saw Box Patterns

Are you curious about how to create stunning band saw boxes? Well, I have got you covered! Keep reading to discover the step-by-step process that I follow to craft these beautiful boxes. Additionally, there 31 unique and one-of-a-kind band saw box patterns that you can follow and create beautiful boxes.

John Traeger

Band Saw Box Patterns

Copyright © 2024 By John Traeger

All rights reserved. No part of this book may be reproduced in any form or by any electronic or mechanical means including storage and retrieval systems without permission in writing from John Traeger. You are free to create and sell or give away as many bandsaw boxes as you'd like using the patterns in this book. However, you are not allowed to copy and sell the copyrighted patterns in this book.

Disclaimer

The patterns in this book are intended to help woodworkers create a Band Saw Box, but they are not a substitute for proper woodworking training. Woodworking involves understanding equipment, proper tool usage, and being aware of environmental factors. It also carries inherent risks. The author and publisher recommend that readers take full responsibility for their safety and understand their own limitations. Before attempting the skills outlined in this book, ensure that your equipment is well-maintained and avoid taking risks beyond your level of experience, skill, training, and comfort.

The process I follow to create bandsaw boxes is simply my preferred method and what works best for me. I want to emphasize that this is not the only way, as each woodworker will develop their own techniques. There are numerous books and videos available on how to make bandsaw boxes, and I encourage you to explore other methods as well. I have included pictures that illustrate the finished bandsaw box. The types of wood I have used can be substituted with any wood of your choice. Many of these designs have received awards at art shows and have garnered positive reviews on my website.

Table of Contents

Patterns	Page
Catalina	39
Splash	42
Wild Bramble	45
Together Forever	48
Bountiful	51
Blissful Sanctum	54
Dew Drops	57
Spherical	60
Breezy Point	63
Spellbound	66
Tempest	69
Twilight	72
Cascade	75
Sea Shell	78
Summer Tree	81
Tea Pot	84
Bristly Virgin	87
Enchanted	90
Windblown	93
The Phantom	96
Majestic Tree	99
Serengeti III	102
Serengeti IV	105
Magnum	108
Lovers	111
Winterberries	114
Skylarker	117
Serengeti VI	120
Prancing Hemlock	123
Free Spirits	126
Reflections	129

Band Saw Box Patterns

As a woodworking artist, my love for woodworking is fueled by two important things: the desire to create beautiful Jewelry Boxes that will last for generations in your family, and the ongoing search for unique, exotic, and domestic wood species with beautiful and unusual grains and color patterns.

For over 30 years, I have focused on developing and creating new ways to improve my woodworking skills. As an active member of the American Association of Wood Turners, Minnesota Woodworkers Guild, and the Minnesota Wood Turners Association, my desire to design and create unique and functional wood art has been enhanced.

In my artistic process, I emphasize the visual aspects of color and contrast in my work while maintaining the natural beauty of the wood material. I use various exotic and domestic hardwoods, striving to blend different woods to form visually attractive combinations. The wood colors you see in my online store are 100% natural; I do not use any stains or dyes to alter what nature has given. I use a wipe-on polyurethane varnish clear coat to enhance the natural wood color and create a finish that will last for generations. The final finish on my work is Renaissance Wax, a light coat of micro-crystalline wax polish that resists liquid spillage and fingerprints.

It brings me profound joy to see people smile when they discover my work at an art fair or in a gallery. I hope that those who own one of my jewelry boxes smile often as they use, handle, or simply glimpse the piece in passing, knowing that it will be in their family for generations. I love conversations about wood, art, woodworking, and the role of craftsmanship in enhancing the human experience. Please feel free to communicate through email or, even better, stop by my booth at an art fair. Thank you for visiting my website, and please like me on Facebook.

Tools and steps I use to make Band Saw Boxes

Note: I make twenty band saw boxes at a time, and I have all of my patterns picked out and sized according to the width of the boards I am working with.

1. **Large Format Printer**: The printer I use is a wide format, this printer will work with the different size papers, Letter, Legal, and Ledger. You will need all of these sizes when working with the different patterns in this book. There are many other brands of printers available it does not matter which on you use, as long as it will print 8 1/2" x 11" letter paper, 8 1/2" x 14" legal paper, and 11" x 17" ledger paper. Also the printer should be able to decrease or increase the size of the pattern, to work with the width of the board you are using. You can adjust the patterns in increments on the printer to get the exact size you want.

Fig. 1

Tools and steps I use to make Band Saw Boxes

2. Jointer: When I need to square up the edge of a board, I use a Jointer to true up the edge. This allows me to achieve a precise and perfect edge to place against the fence of the table saw. This ensures that I can cut the board to the exact width required for the pattern I am working with and achieve the best results possible. The Jointer is a useful tool that helps me ensure that my woodworking projects are successful and of the highest quality.

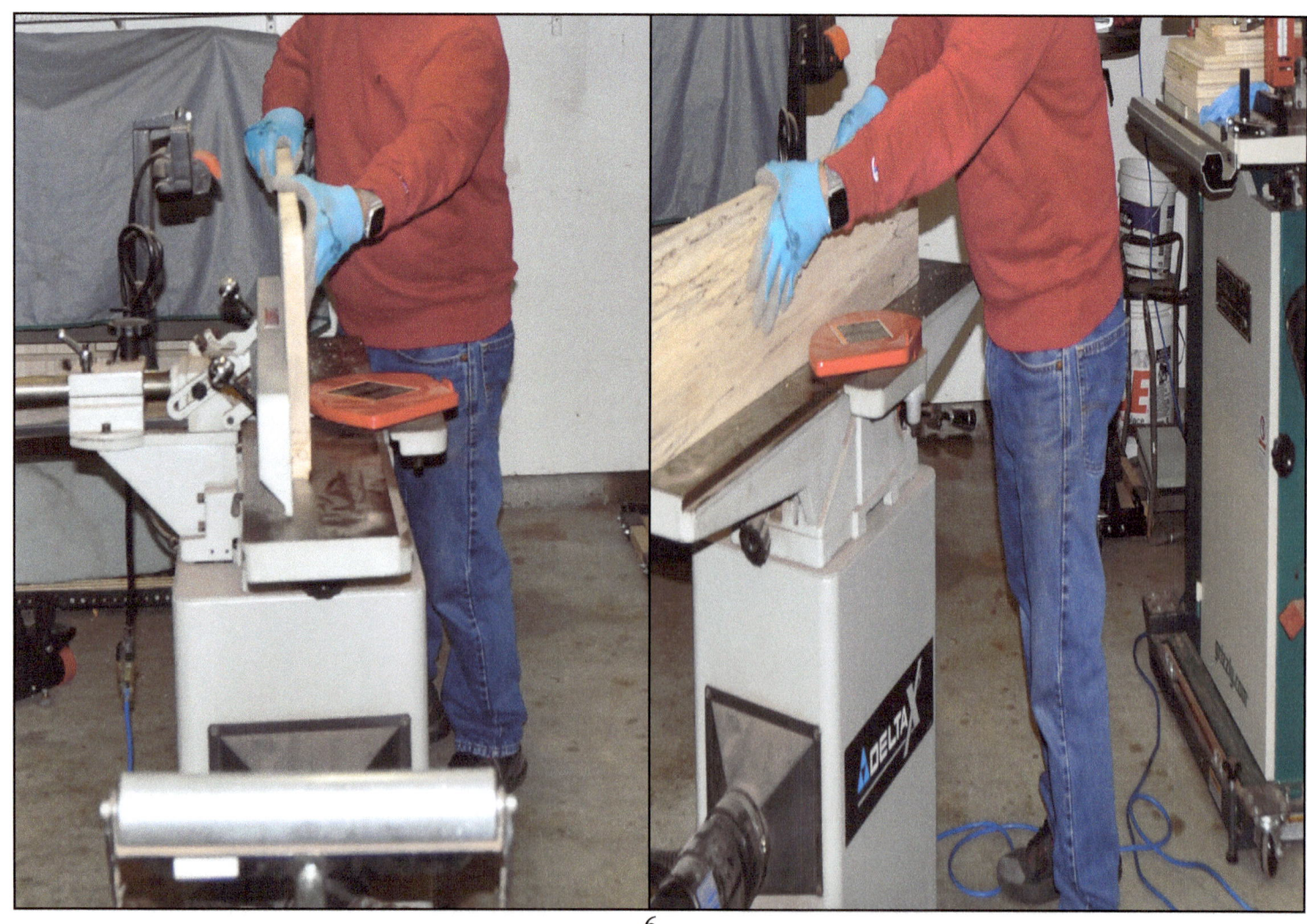

Tools and steps I use to make Band Saw Boxes

3. **Planner**: In order to ensure that the boards I am working with have a perfectly flat surface, I draw lines across both sides of the board as shown in Fig. 2a. Once the lines are completely removed from the board, the surface of both sides of the board become perfectly squared up, which ensures that there will be no gaps when I glue the boards together to form a block for the box.

Tools I use to make Band Saw Boxes

5. **Table Saw**: After running the boards through the planer, I use the table saw to cut them to the necessary width for the patterns I am working with.

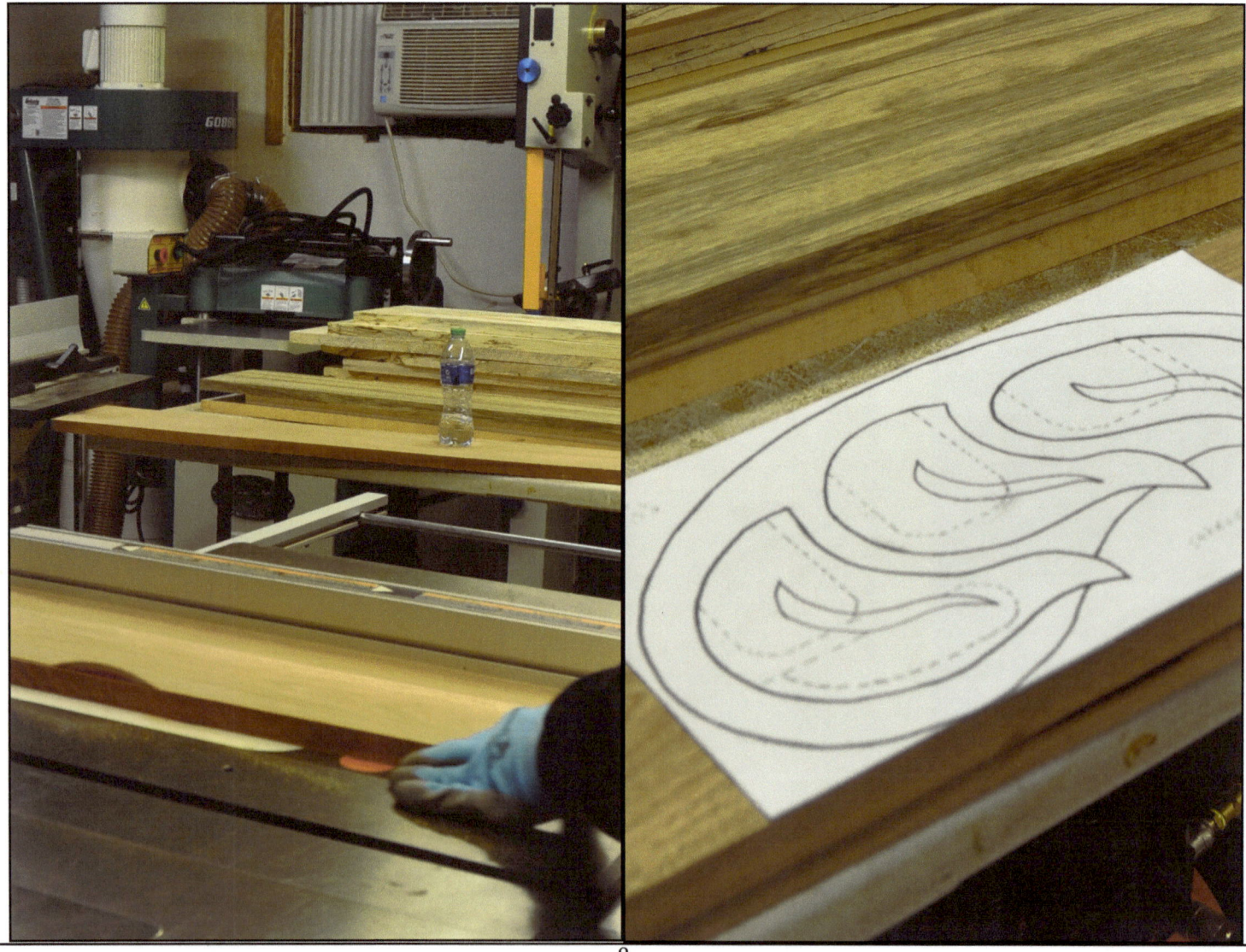

Tools and steps I use to make Band Saw Boxes

5. **Miter Saw**: I use a miter saw to cut a board into the required width for the pattern I am working on. I had already decided on the length of the cut and the number of boards I would need to form a block of wood for the box. To make the process more efficient, I set up a stop on the miter box, which allowed me to make continuous cuts until I had the required number of boards for the block.

Tools and steps I use to make Band Saw Boxes

6. **Glue and Clamps:** After cutting the boards to the desired width for the patterns, the next step is to glue them together to form a block for the box. I prefer to use Titebond II wood glue as it has been effective for me. Once the boards are glued up, I use a Tri-Square and a piece of scrap wood to continually square up the block until it stops shifting, as shown in Fig 6b. After the block has set up for several minutes, I clamp it. I've noticed that if the block is clamped right after applying the glue, the boards tend to slide around during the clamping process.

Tools and steps I use to make Band Saw Boxes

7. **Band Saw:** Once the boards are glued together to form a block for the box, in the next step I cut the back of the box off. To determine which side of the block should be the front of the box, I looked for the side with the most interesting wood grain. Then, I used a Band Saw to re-saw around 1/4" from the block of wood. This cut will create the back of the box.

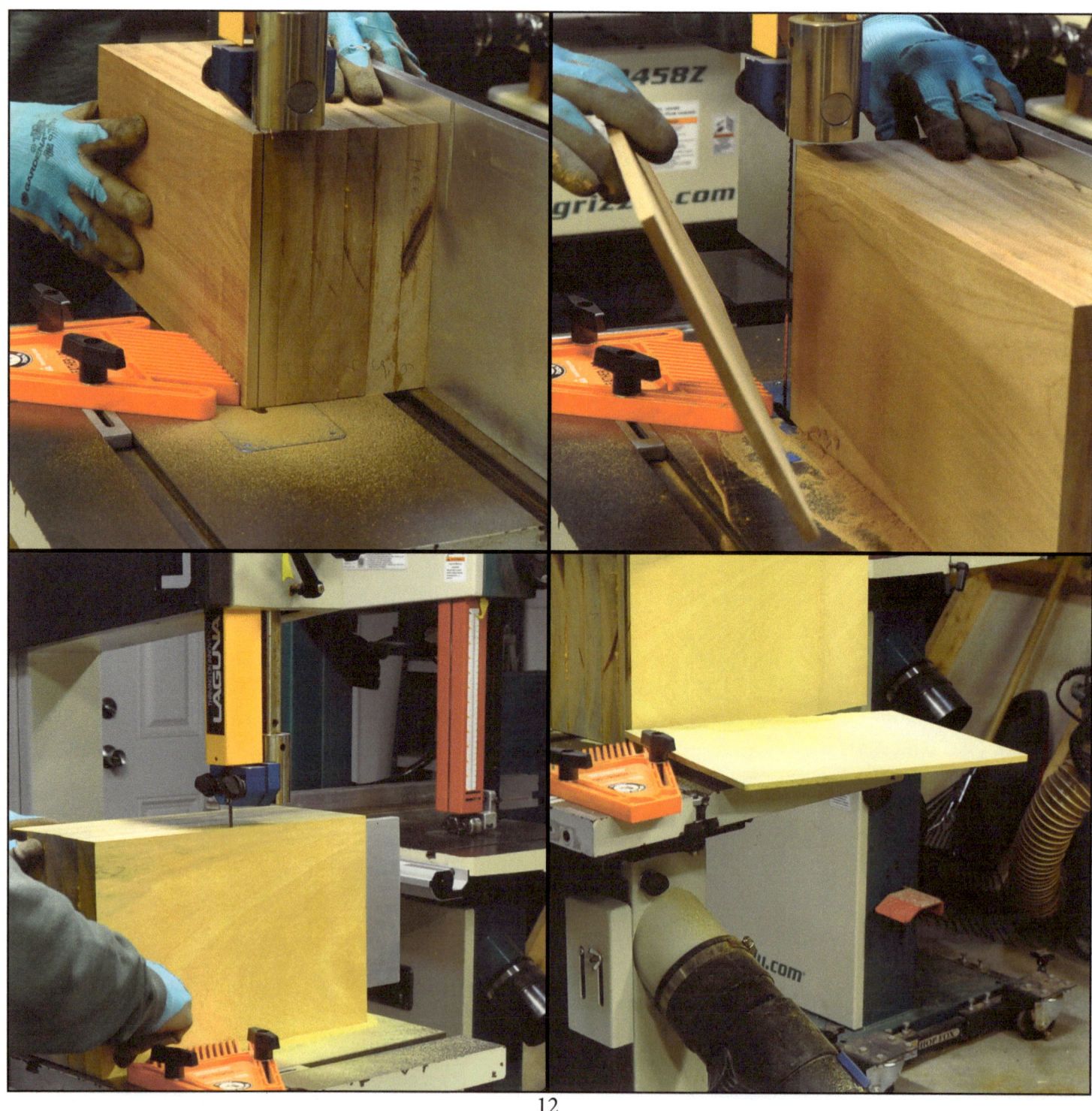

Tools and steps I use to make Band Saw Boxes

8. **Spray Adhesive:** After cutting off the backs of the boxes, the next step is to place the patterns on the face of the wooden block. I apply a light coat of spray adhesive to the back of the pattern before placing it on the block. It's important to make sure the surface of the block is free of dust particles before applying the pattern. If the pattern is difficult to remove, a heat gun or hair dryer can be used to make the process easier.

Tools and steps I use to make Band Saw Boxes

9. **Band Saw:** Now that the patterns have been attached to the block, using my band saw, it is time to cut out the drawers. Make sure not to force the blade to cut; instead, let it glide through the wood with a nice, steady and slow feed. Always stay on the line, and the drawer will come out perfect. Also, before starting the cut, it's essential to determine the exact entry point. I use a 3/16th 10 TPI rake tooth blade and a 3/16th skip tooth 4 TPI for cutting the drawers and the outside shape of the box. I purchased these blades at Union Grove Saw & Knife Inc.

Tools and steps I use to make Band Saw Boxes

10. Clamps: Now that the drawers have been removed from the box, the next step is to glue the back of the box onto the block. If you need to sand the inside of the drawer cavities now is the time before the back is glued on. You need to ensure that the outside edges are flush with each other. Sometimes, you may need to widen the saw blade cuts by inserting shims into them. For this purpose, sheet metal strips can be used. Alternatively, you may have to put a shim inside the drawer cavities to adjust the blade width cut. After cutting out the drawers, I don't immediately glue the back on. Instead, I let the box rest for 24 hours. This is because I've noticed that the box can shift slightly during this time. If the saw gap is wider than the blade cut, the next day the box will have adjusted itself. After clamping the back to the box, remove the excess glue from inside the drawer cavities before it dries. You may need to be creative to do this.

Tools and steps I use to make Band Saw Boxes

11. Band Saw: Now that the back of the box has been glued back onto it, it's time to cut the outside shape of the pattern from the block of wood. Before starting to cut, observe the block of wood to determine the best way to begin and the potential changes in the cutting process that might be needed to complete the outside shape of the box. Remember to feed the box steadily into the blade with a slow and smooth motion. Also, a dull blade is not your friend.

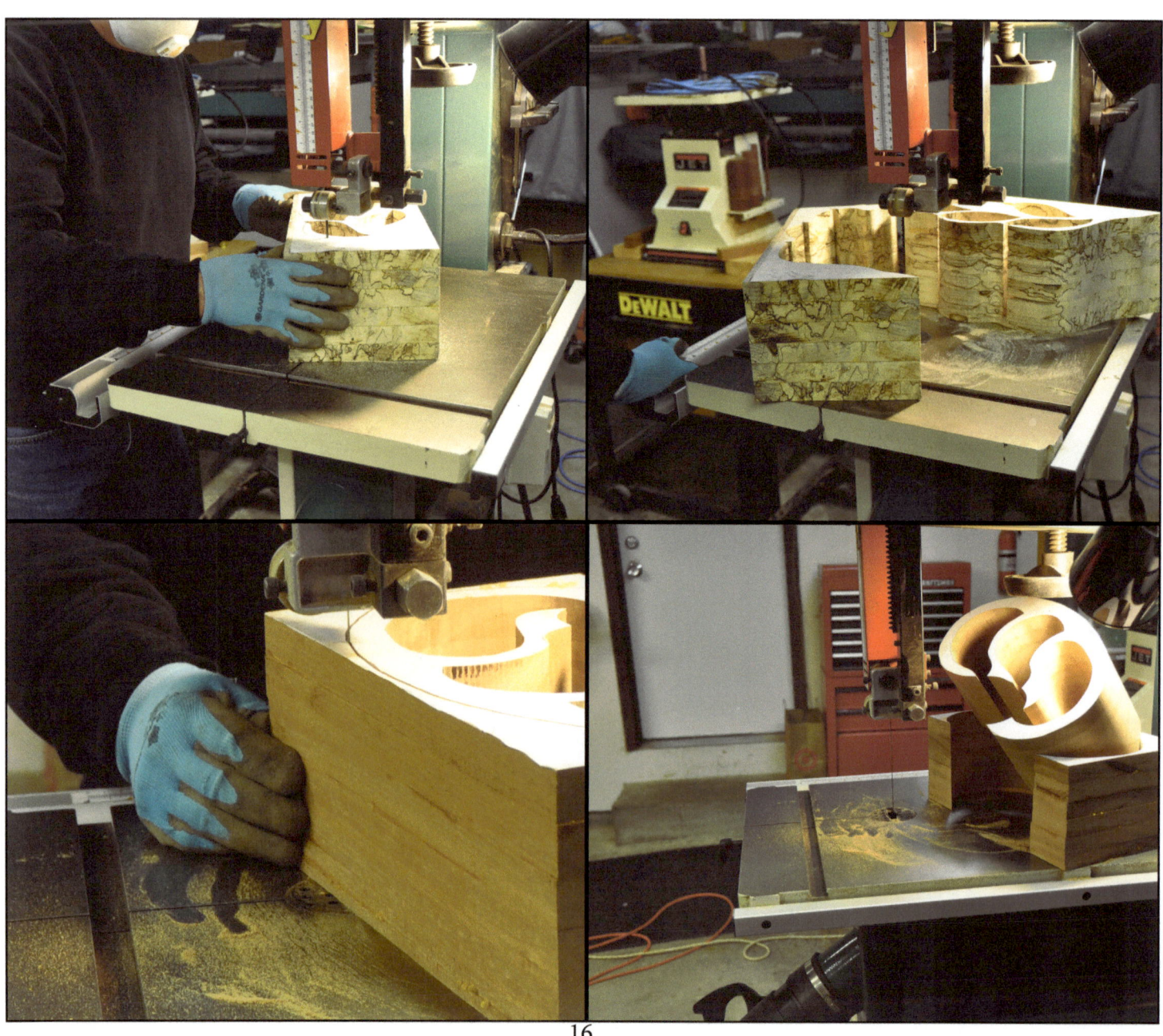

Tools and steps I use to make Band Saw Boxes

12. Band Saw: Drawer Construction; I've made a decision about what I want to do with the drawers. If you look at the pictures of the Band Saw Boxes in this book, you'll notice that the drawers stick out a little from the box. I like that look. However, it does require some extra work. If you don't want that look for your boxes, you can just construct the drawers the standard way. You can do this by cutting the front and back of the drawer off, then cutting the drawer cavities out and gluing the front and back on.

Below are pictures of the steps I take when I keep the same wood for the front of the drawer. I leave the front of the drawer as is and create a new back out of the same board or the same wood. When using this method, do not cut the back of the drawer off, only the front. The piece you traced and cut will become the new back of the box. After cutting the drawer cavities, you can glue the front and new back on. Note: If you are going to cut out the secret drawer, refer to the secret drawer instructions in this book.

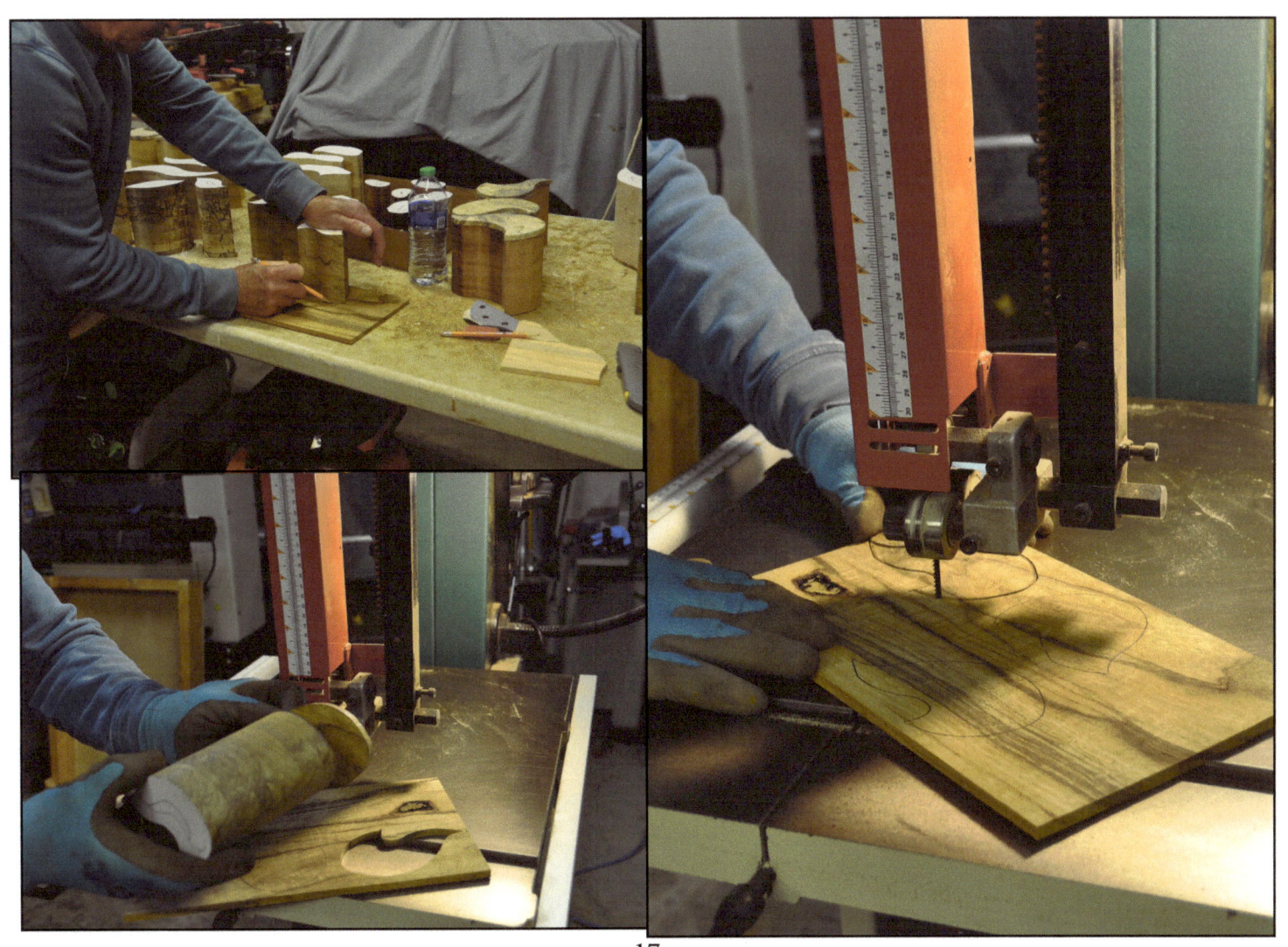

Tools and steps I use to make Band Saw Boxes

13. **Band Saw: Drawer Construction;** If you plan to add a different wood to the front of the drawer, start by tracing the drawer front onto the accent wood. Cut the traced wood just outside of the traced line, and then do some sanding after gluing it onto the drawer front. Important: Don't cut out the drawer cavities before tracing the drawer front onto the accent wood. If you plan to cut out a secret drawer go to the instructions on secret drawers in this book.

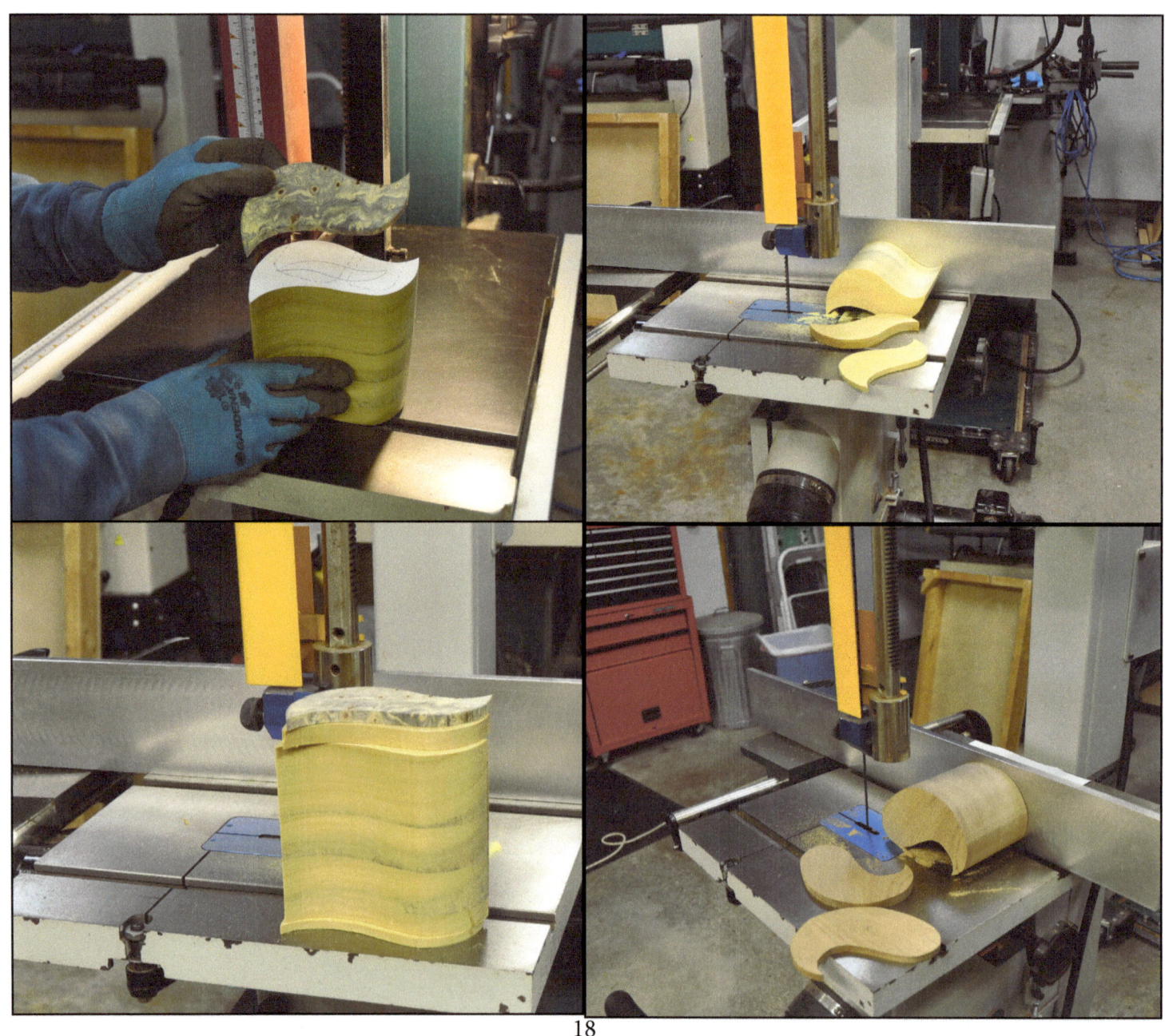

Tools and steps I use to make Band Saw Boxes

14. Drawer Construction: Now that I have cut the front and back of the drawers, it's time to remove the drawer cavities on the bandsaw. Remember, a dull blade is not your friend. Also, maintain a slow, steady feed as you glide through the cutout.

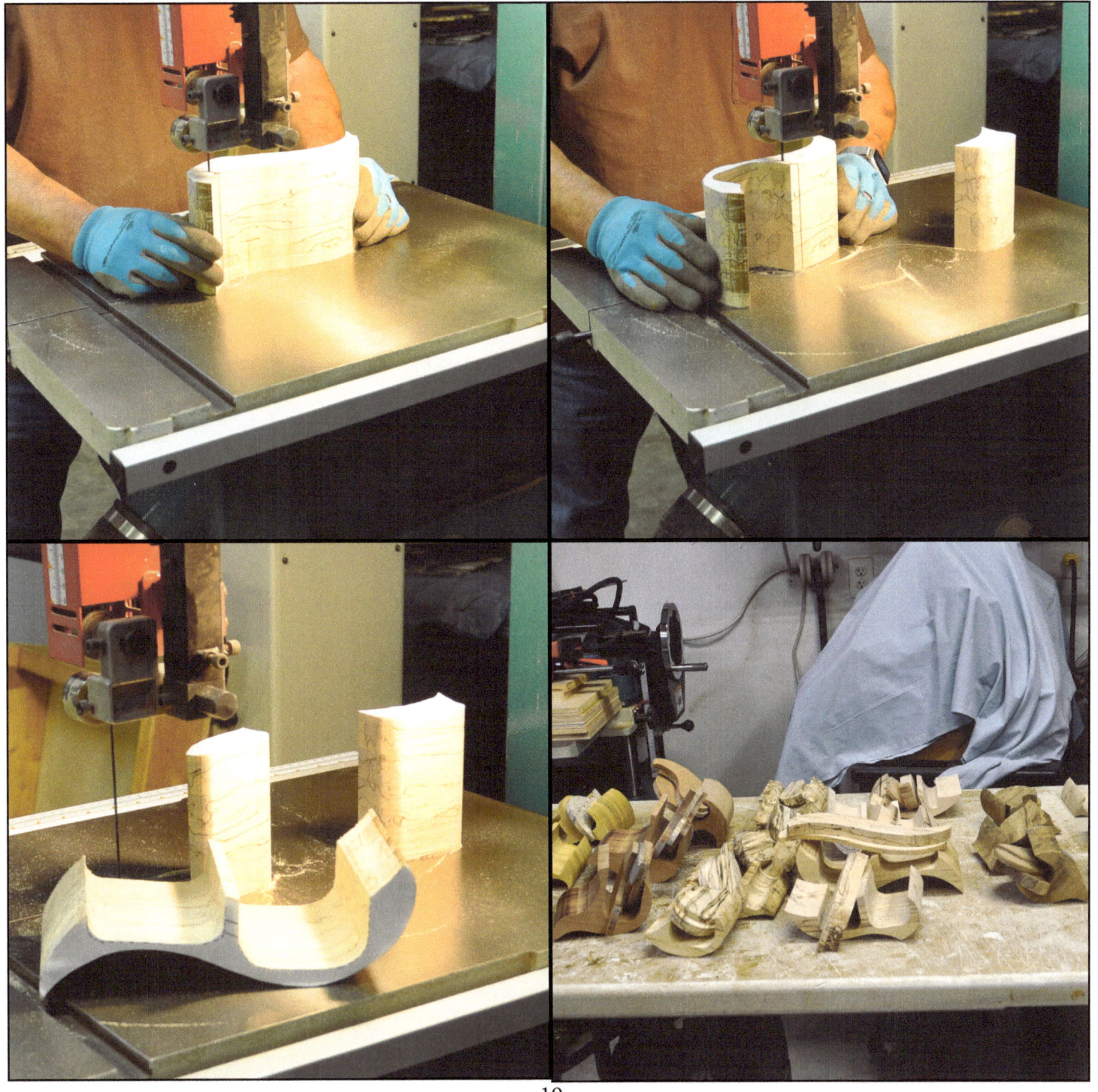

Tools and steps I use to make Band Saw Boxes

15. Oscillating Spindle Sander: I have now cut out the drawer cavities, so it's time to use the spindle sander. I use the spindle sander to smooth out the inside of the drawer cavities. This way, when I finish the inside of the drawers with flocking, any saw cuts will not show up after the flocking is applied.

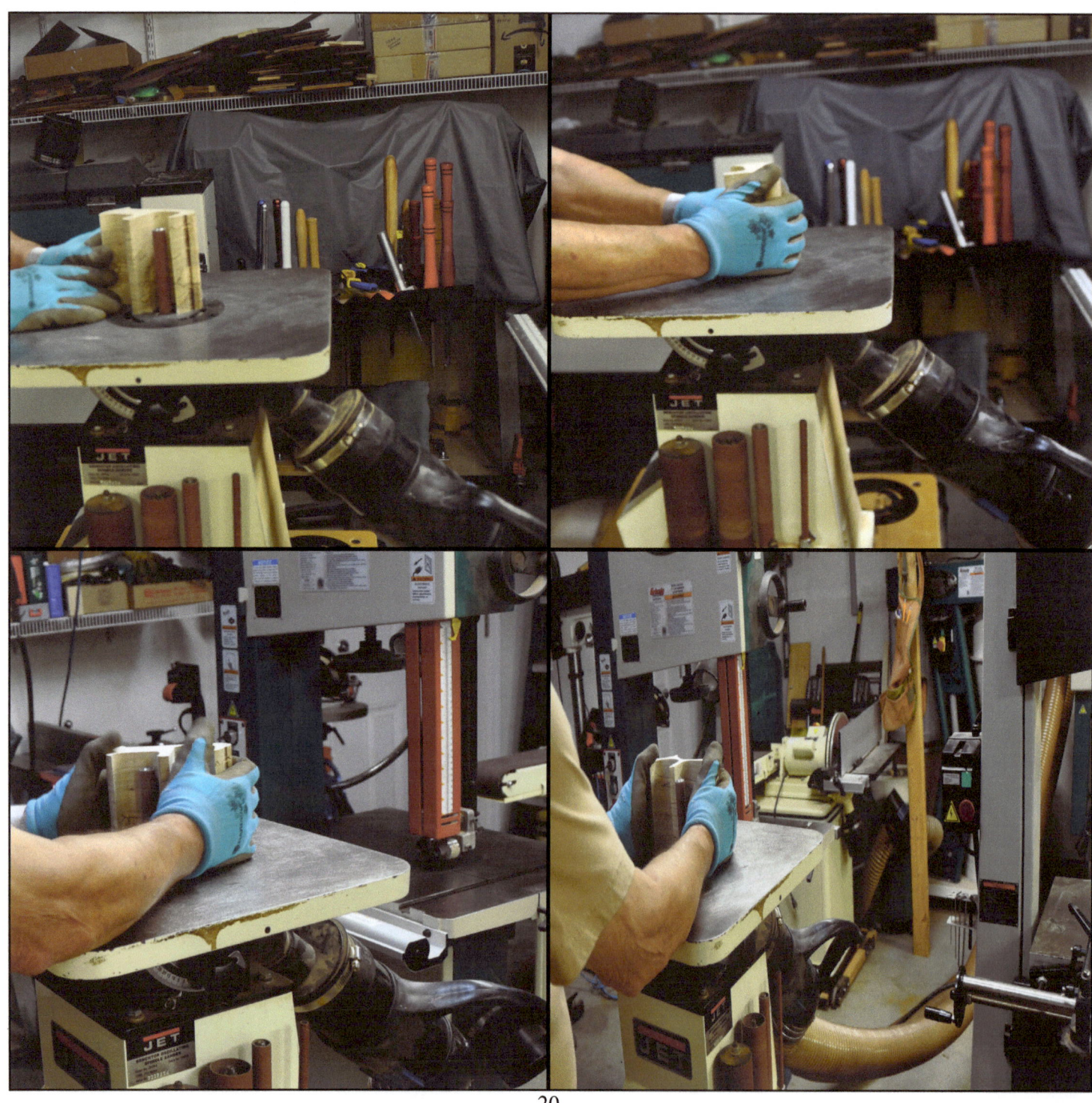

Tools and steps I use to make Band Saw Boxes

16. Drawer Construction: Now that I have the front and back of the drawer cut and the drawer cavities cut out, I start to glue the drawers back together. After gluing the front and back pieces to the drawer, I let it set for several minutes to allow the glue to set up before clamping. The parts might shift a little, so it's important to keep aligning the parts so they are flush with the drawer. Be sure to clean any glue squeeze-out inside and outside the drawer. Note: To create a secret drawer, first glue the back of the drawer, then cut out the secret compartment. Next, glue and clamp the drawer where the secret compartment cut was made, and finally glue the front of the drawer back on. "For more information, please refer to the article about the secret drawer in this book."

Tools and steps I use to make Band Saw Boxes

17. **Secret Drawers:** When I start the process of cutting the secret drawers, the first thing I do is put a new bandsaw blade on the bandsaw. Also, I make sure the tension on the blade is correct. Then I cut the drawer out with a slow, steady feed through the blade. I do not force the cut.

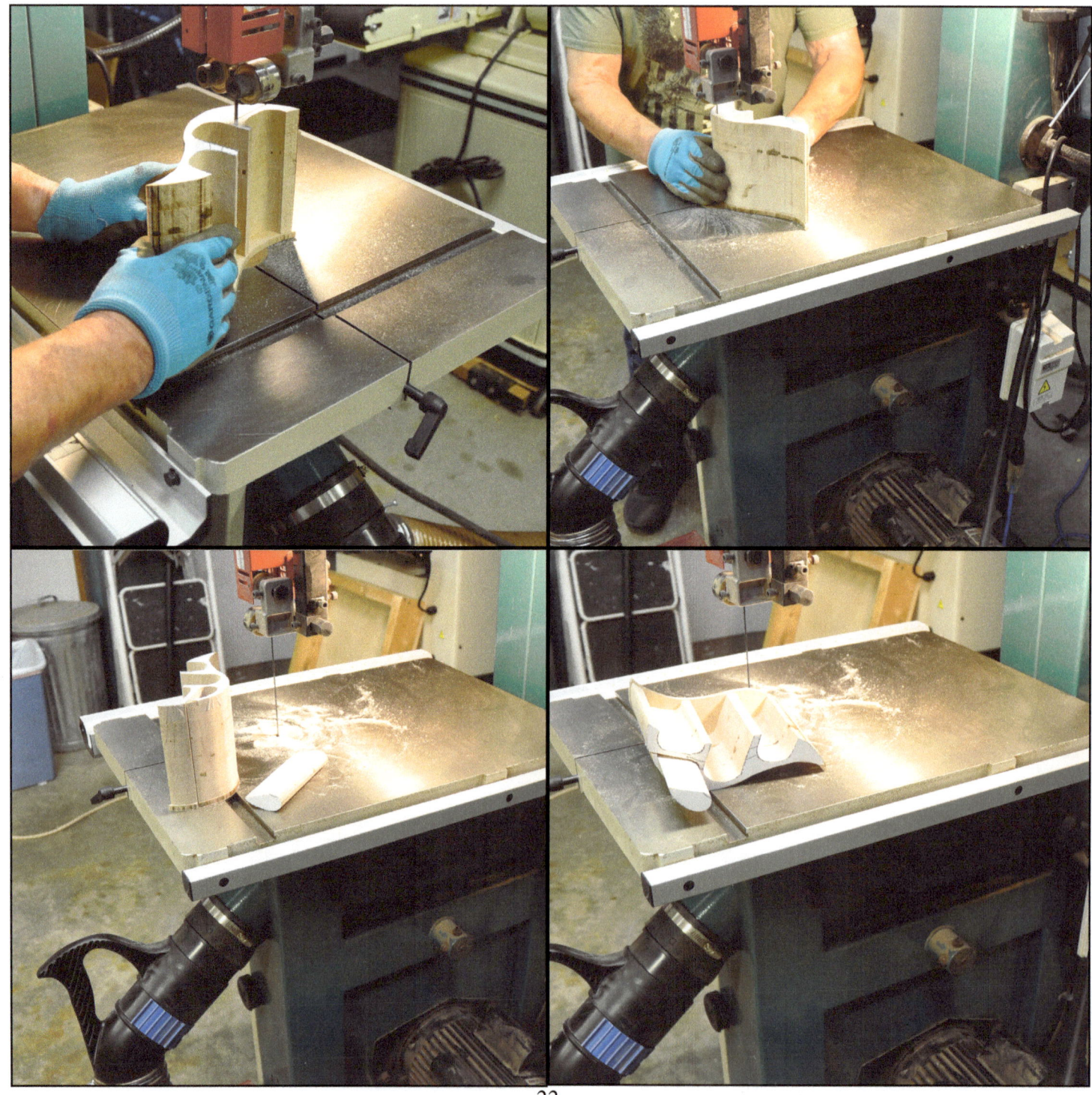

Tools and steps I use to make Band Saw Boxes

18. Secret Drawers: Now that I have the secret drawers cut out, it's time to glue up the entry cut that was made by cutting out the secret drawer. Before you glue, it is a good idea to do a pre-clamp to determine how you are going to clamp after you glue. Sometimes, you have to get creative with the clamping, so you should already have that figured out before you glue. Also, be careful there may be some weak points in the box when you clamp. After clamping cleanup glue both inside and outside of the secret drawer cavity. Proceed making the secret drawer the same way you would a regular drawer.

Tools and steps I use to make Band Saw Boxes

19. Belt Sander & Spindle Sander: After finishing the drawers, I begin the sanding process. I use a 6" x 48" belt sander with a 120 grit sanding belt to remove as many of the blade marks as possible. For drawers with a new back, I focus on sanding that side until it is flush with the box, and then proceed to sand the rest of the box. Additionally, I use a spindle sander to reach areas that the belt sander can't. I take care not to change the original shape of the drawer while sanding.

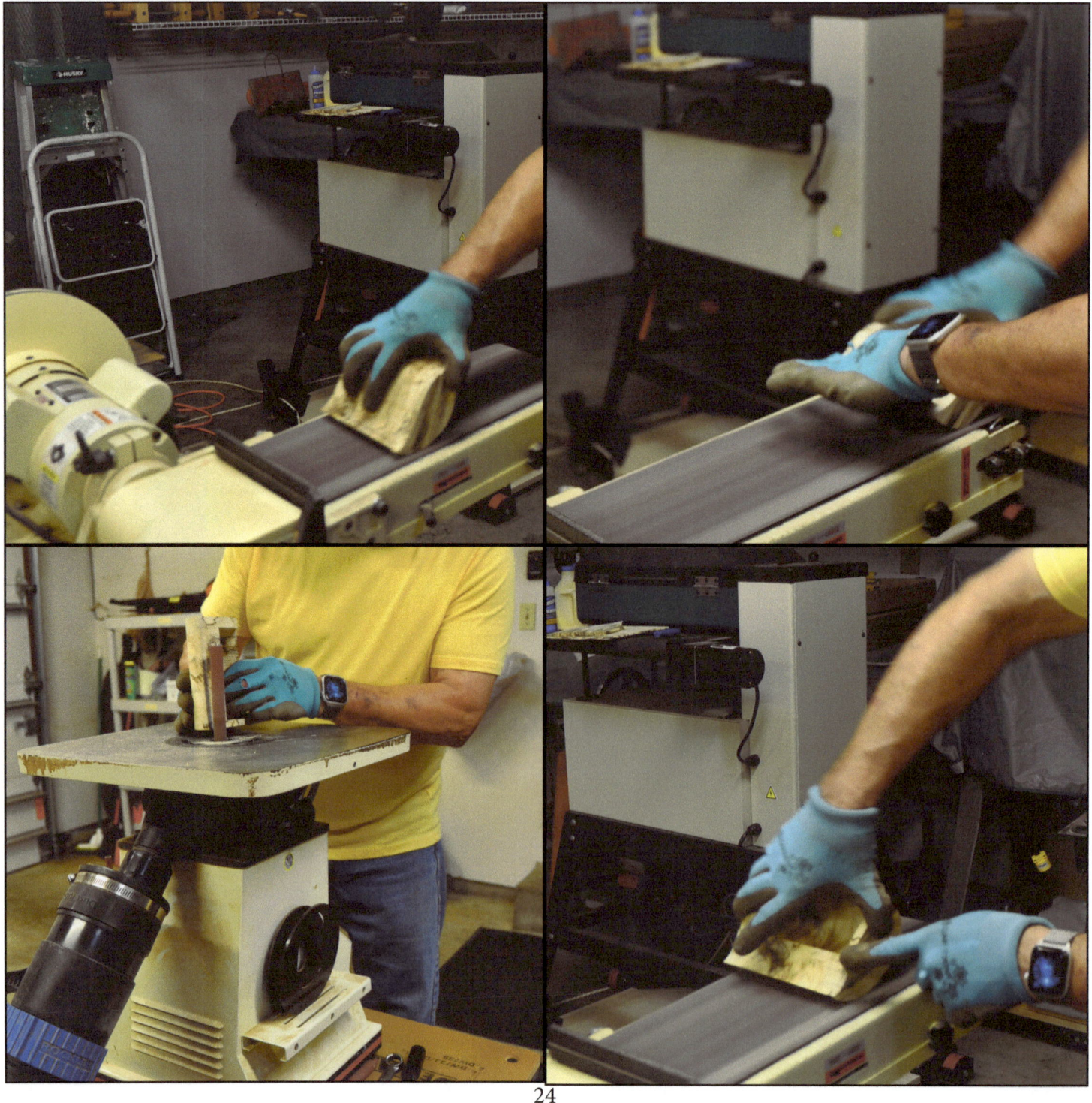

Tools and steps I use to make Band Saw Boxes

20. Belt Sander & Spindle Sander: After finishing the drawers, I move on to the main box and sand out the blade marks using the belt sander and spindle sander. I make sure the bottom of the box is sanded smooth so that it will sit properly on a table. During the sanding process of both the drawers and the box make sure to stay true to the original design of the pattern.

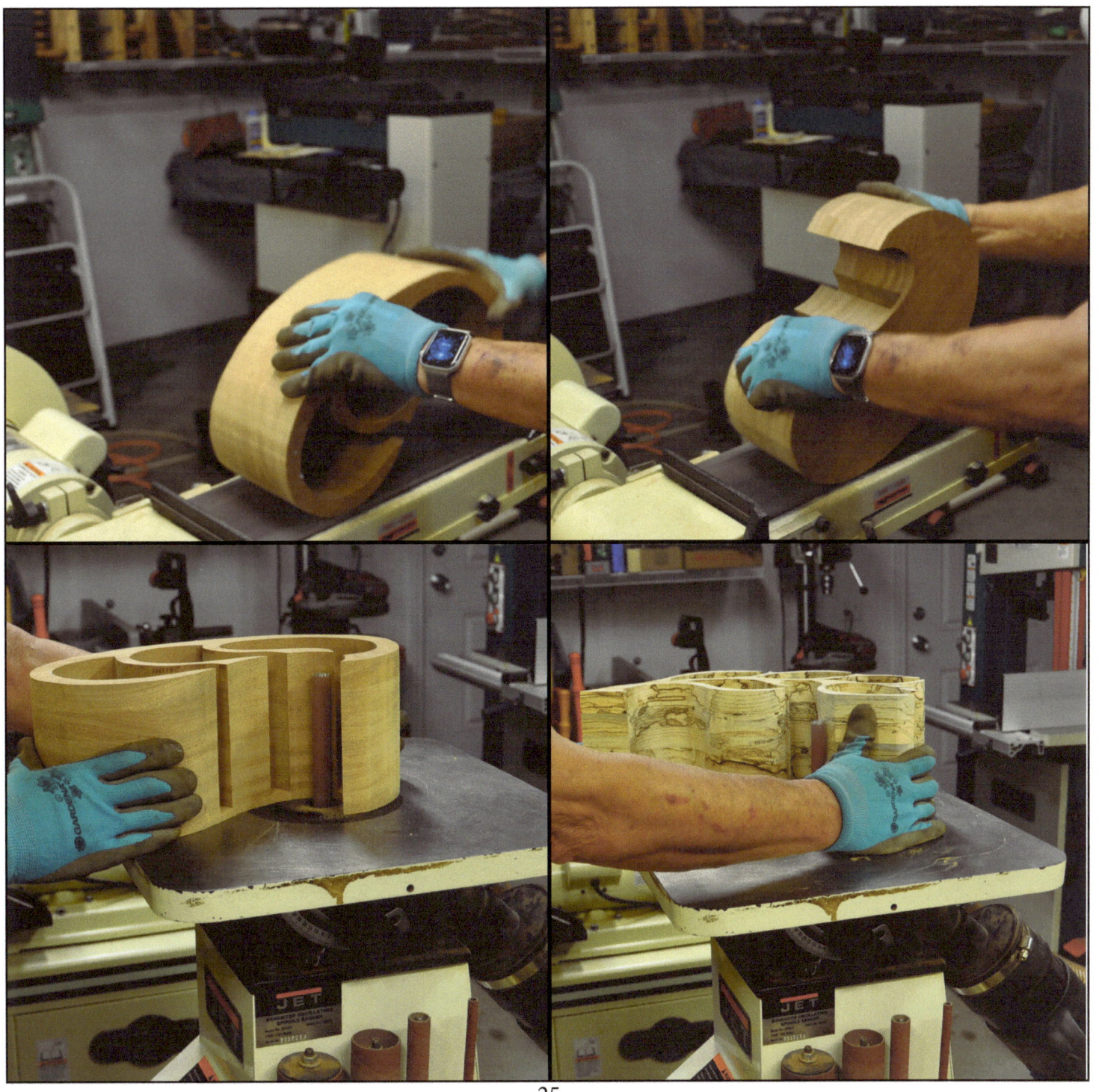

Tools and steps I use to make Band Saw Boxes

21. Making Drawer Pulls: I need to make the drawer pulls. First, I check the pattern diagram to see what the handles should look like. If it's a new box, I create a pattern drawer handle using 1/4" plywood or any available wood scraps. This pattern will help me make the drawer pulls in the future. Drawer pulls are a matter of personal preference, so feel free to design your own style of handles. I prefer using wood types that create a beautiful contrast of grains and colors to enhance the box's appearance.

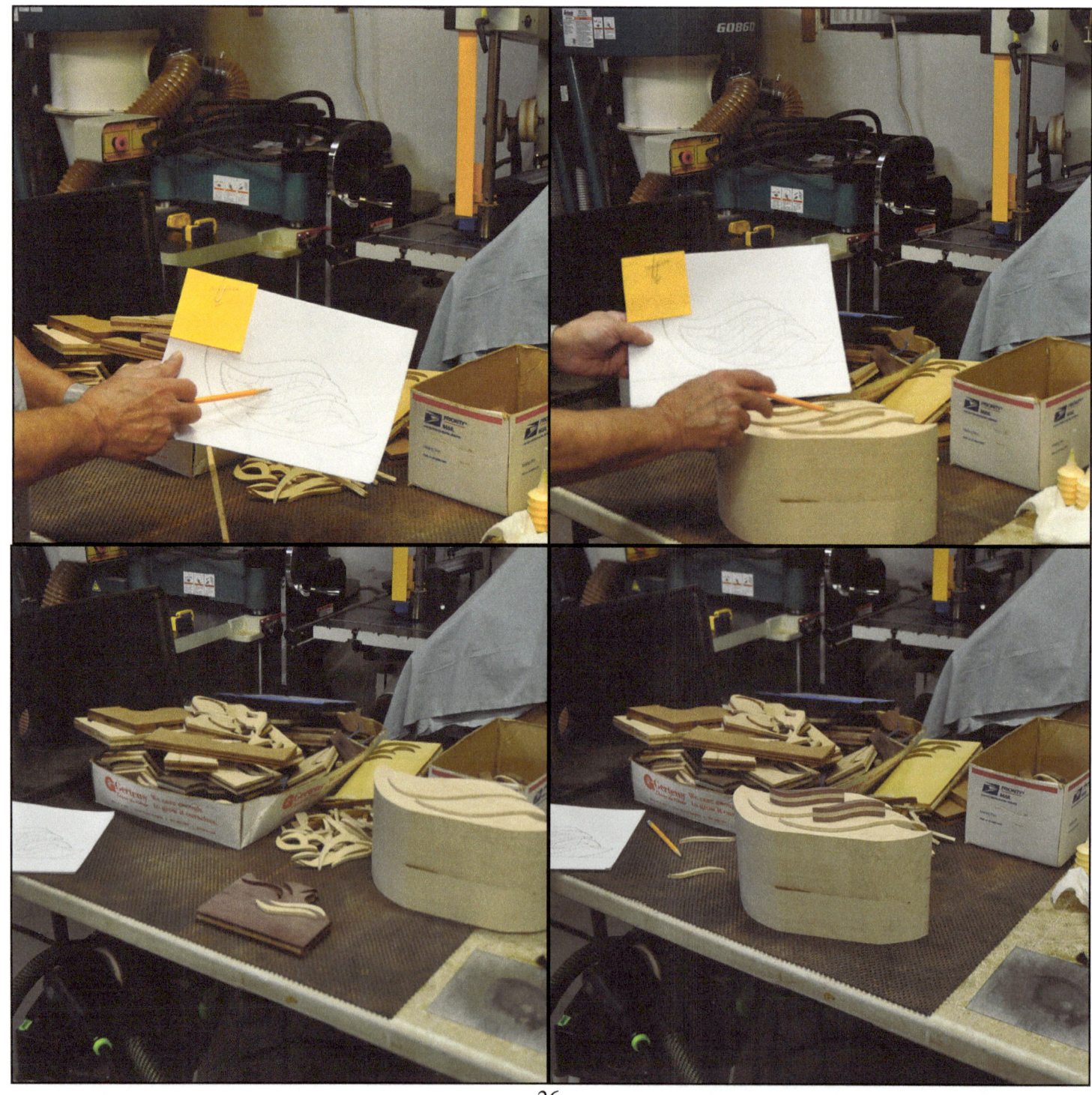

Tools and steps I use to make Band Saw Boxes

22. Spindle Sander & Belt Sander: I use the spindle sander, belt sander, and hand sanding to fine-tune the drawer pulls. This is the point where I finalize the shape of the drawer pulls. Although the drawer pulls have their final shape, they still need to be sanded through the grits. I typically stop at around 400 grit, but do whatever you are comfortable with.

Tools and steps I use to make Band Saw Boxes

23. **Palm Sander:** After rough sanding the boxes and drawers with 120 grit on the belt sander, I proceed to use the palm sander with 150 grit sanding discs. There will be areas of the boxes and drawers that cannot be reached with the palm sander, so I have to do some hand sanding. Sometimes I have to get creative with the hand sanding.

Tools and steps I use to make Band Saw Boxes

24. Router Table: After finishing the rough sanding with the 150 grit, I take the boxes to the router table. I start by using a 1/8" round-over bit to route out all the edges of the box, both inside and out. Then, I focus on routing the drawers on the outside edges only. When routing the drawers, I stop at a 1/8" round-over on the back of the drawer.

After using the 1/8" bit, I switch to the 3/16" round-over bit and repeat the process. Now, I have to use my judgment to decide when to stop routing in certain areas of the box. Then, I continue moving up through the different round-over bits (1/4", 5/16", 3/8") until I achieve the desired look. I don't use a round-over bit larger than 3/8" unless there's enough wood to support the cut.

Note: Make sure there is always enough wood to support the router bit cut, or you can disfigure the box or drawer. I strongly recommend using a router table to round over the edges of the box and drawers. Remember on a router table, you rotate the outside edges counter-clockwise on the box and drawers and clockwise for the inside edges of the box.

Tools and steps I use to make Band Saw Boxes

25. Sanding & Drawer Pulls: After completing the router work, the next step involves additional sanding. I meticulously sand through the various grit levels until I achieve the desired smoothness and appearance for the box. Now it time to glue the drawer pulls onto the drawers, the first thing I do is position the pulls exactly where I want them before adding the glue. Then I glue the pull and try and place it where it was. I do not clamp the pull I just let them sit overnight and they are good to go.

Tools and steps I use to make Band Saw Boxes

26. Finishing The Bandsaw Box: Now that I've attached the drawer pulls to the drawers, it's time to finish the boxes. I begin by applying a first coat of shellac to the box and drawers, inside and out, and then move on to applying an oil-based wipe-on polyurethane. For more details, please read the finishing article in this book. "I finish my boxes this way, but feel free to use any wood finish that suits your preferences."

Tools and steps I use to make Band Saw Boxes

28. Self-Adhesive Velvet Sheets: When I first began crafting bandsaw boxes, I encountered an issue with the scraping sound the drawers made when I opened them. I found a solution by purchasing a 12" x 24" sheet of self-adhesive velvet and cutting it into 1/4" x 4" strips. I then placed these strips in the areas where the drawers were scraping against the wood, which not only eliminated the sound but also enhanced the visual arrangement of the drawers. If you're interested in trying this out, you can find the self-adhesive velvet at woodworking store.

Tools and steps I use to make Band Saw Boxes

29. Flocking The Drawers: I apply flocking inside the drawers to give the box a more finished look. If you're interested in trying this, you can find all the flocking supplies at your woodworking store or online. They offer a variety of colors to choose from. When brushing the glue into the drawer cavities, I keep some mineral spirits nearby in case I get any glue outside of the drawer. Just a little on a rag will remove the glue without damaging the finish. Once you have the flocking sprayed on let the drawer set for 24 to 48 hours the remove the excess flocking and your all set.

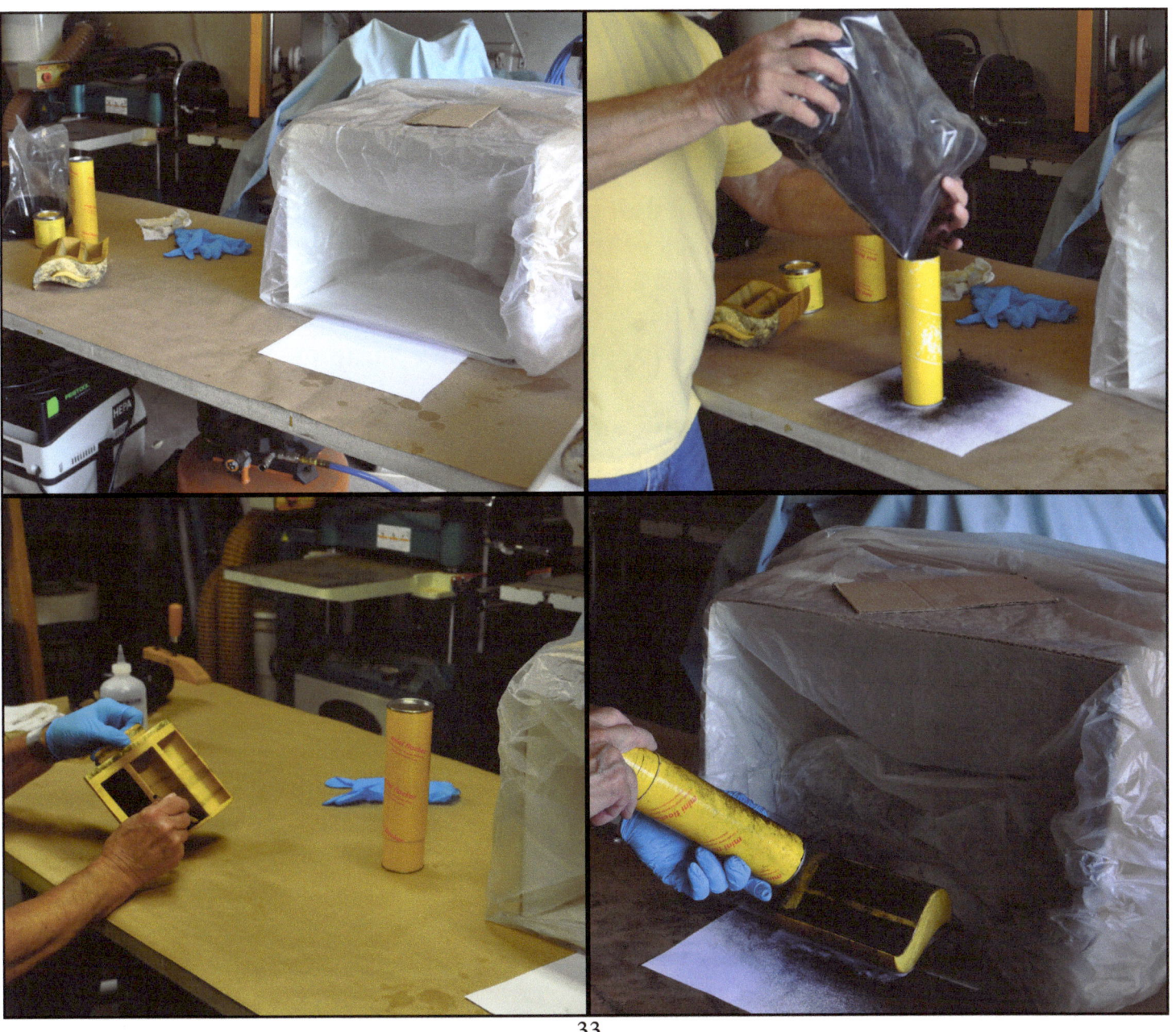

Secret Drawers

Sequence for cutting out the secret drawers: When the block of wood is glued up, I first cut or re-saw the back of the box. Then, I applied 3M spray adhesive (a very light coat) to the back of the pattern and attached the pattern to the block of wood. You want to apply a light coat of the adhesive so you can easily peel off the drawer pattern and reapply later. Note: If the pattern is difficult to remove, try using a heat gun or hair dryer. It will come off very easily. So, after you cut off the back of the box, you are ready to cut out the drawers. After the drawers are cut out, you must decide what you will do with the drawer fronts. There are three options.

1. If you do not plan on adding an accent wood to the drawer front, the drawer will be flush with the box. In this case, you can cut the front and back of the drawer off of the drawer blank. Then, take the pattern and use scotch tape to attach it back onto the drawer. Cut out the drawer cavities and then glue the back of the drawer back on, not the front, as it will become the secret drawer stop. Once the back of the drawer is glued, you are ready to cut the secret drawer. Simply follow the pattern and take your time with the cut. It's important to use a new blade to cut the secret drawers because a dull blade will not work. Be extremely careful when cutting off the front and back of the secret drawer and cutting the drawer cavity. Remember to use a slow feed and a sharp blade, and have patience. Once you have created a few secret drawers, you will become more confident in your ability to make them. It might be wise to practice on a scrap piece of wood.

2. The next option is when you want to add different or accent wood to the front of the drawer. For example, if the main box is walnut and you wish to put Birdseye maple on the drawer fronts, First, cut the drawers out, and before you cut the drawer cavities out, trace the drawers' outline onto the Birdseye maple. Then, cut the back and front of the drawer off. Once that is complete, cut out the drawer cavities and glue the front and back of the drawer back onto the drawer. You are then ready to cut out the secret drawer. The Birdseye maple becomes the front of the drawer and acts as the secret drawer stop. When cutting the trace line of the Birdseye Maple, cut just the outside of the line; once it is glued to the main drawer front, you can sand flush to the walnut drawer front. This method will allow the drawer fronts to be proud of the main box by whatever thickness of the accent wood. I usually keep it at around 1/4" or 5/16".

3. The following method is used when you want to create drawers that stick out slightly from the main box, around 1/4" or 5/16". To do this, you should use the same wood type for the drawers as the main box, preferably from the same board or wood species. Choose the best-looking woodgrain for the drawer and re-saw it to about 3/8". Then, use a planner or sandpaper to smooth out the cut marks. This piece of wood will become the back of the box.

Next, trace the drawer blanks onto the board, but cut just outside of the line to ensure that the new drawer back is slightly larger than the drawer blank. Cut the front of the drawer off, not the back, and attach the drawer pattern to the drawer blank. Cut out the drawer cavities and glue the new back of the drawer on.

After that, cut out the secret drawer by following the pattern carefully. It's essential to use a new blade for this step because a dull blade won't work. When cutting off the front and back of the secret drawer and cutting the drawer cavity, be extremely careful and use a slow feed and a sharp blade. Remember to have patience, and it might be wise to practice on a scrap piece of wood.

Once the secret drawer is cut out, glue on the front of the drawer. This becomes the stop for the secret drawer. With practice, you'll become more confident in your ability to make secret drawers.

I hope this helps with the secret drawers, if you have any questions be sure and let me know.

Email: jctraeger@live.com or
Call 651-253-1382

Best Regards
John

The Finishing Process I Use

The finish I use for my boxes involves many steps, starting with sanding. I begin with 120-grit sandpaper on my belt sander, then switch to my palm sander, working through the grits from 150 to 600 grit. I also do a lot of hand sanding along the way. If your box has deep bandsaw blade marks, you should start with 80-grit sandpaper and work your way through the grits. Sanding is an essential part of the overall finish.

Once all the sanding is complete, I mix up a 2lb cut of dewaxed super blonde shellac that I make myself and apply it to the entire box. I use spray shellac for the box cavities to make the process faster. On oilier woods, I add several coats of shellac, so the varnish will dry when I apply oil-based woods. After the shellac, I use Minwax High Gloss Polyurethane oil-based finish and apply 4 to 5 coats, depending on the wood I work with. I apply this with a lint-free cotton cloth. I usually buy a bag of rags and cut them up into 6" x 7" pieces. I make sure I have many on hand throughout the process. After cutting the rags, I run them through the clothes washer to remove as much lint as possible. To apply the finish, I use two fingers and a rag.

Between coats, I sand with a 220-sanding sponge about 1/4" thick and make a very light pass with the sponge. The final coat is Renaissance Wax. This wax has the ability to dry hard instantly, resist liquid spillage, not show finger marks, freshen colors, and impart a soft sheen. Renaissance Wax Polish was developed by the British Museum in the early 1950s for fine art conservation. The polish is a blend of highly refined micro-crystalline fossil-origin waxes. To use, simply wipe it on and then buff it off. Also when you apply the wax to the bandsaw box drawers, you will notice that the drawers slide more easily as you pull them in and out.
The finishing process that I use suits my needs. However, many finishing products are available, and the finishing process is a personal preference. So, you can finish your boxes the way you think is best for you.

I hope this helps. If you have any questions, let me know.

Best Regards
John

Artistry In Woodworking

Catalina

This box was handcrafted with African Kiaat and African Padauk for the drawer pull

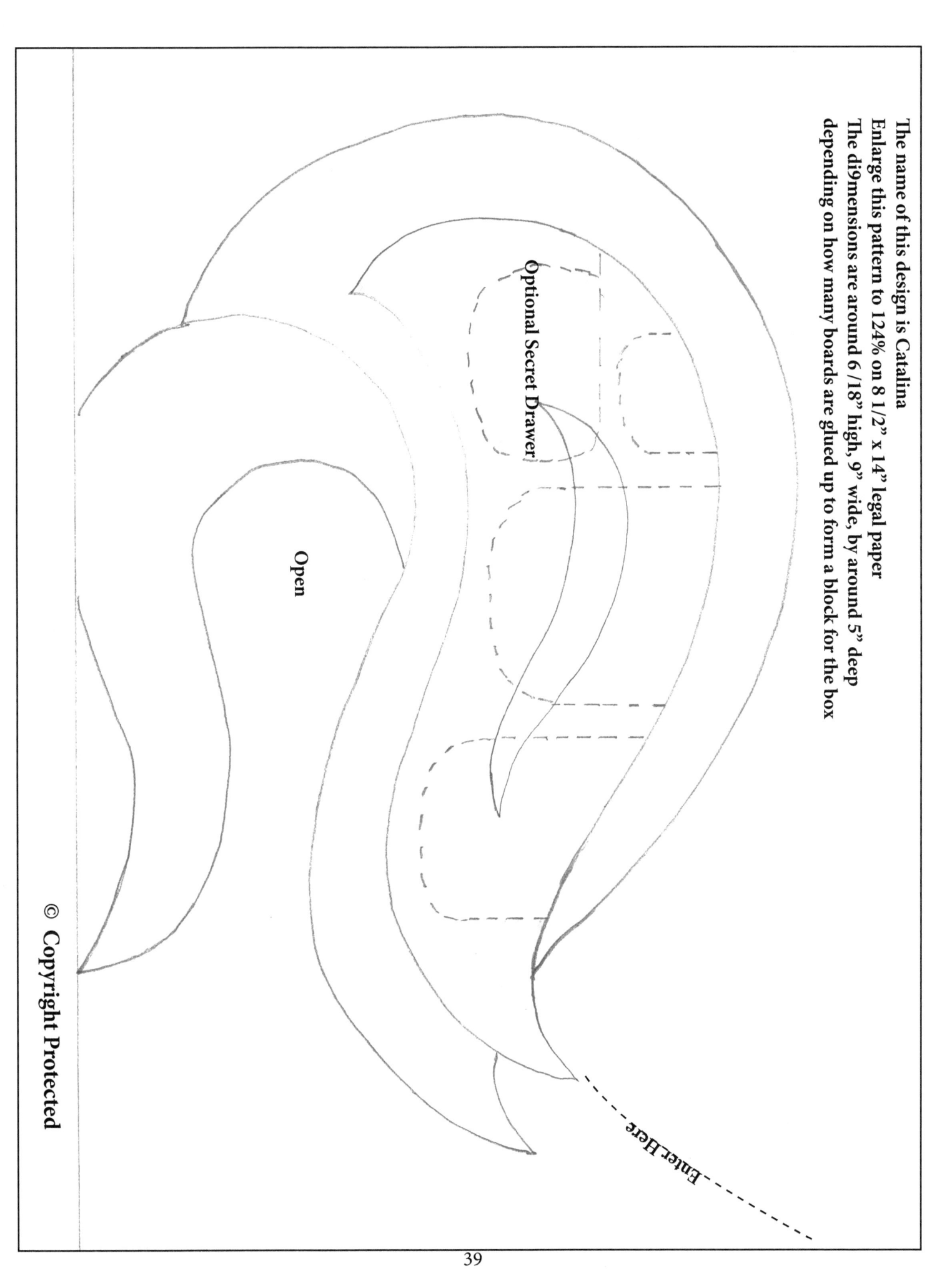

Artistry In Woodworking

Splash

This box was handcrafted with
African Kiaat and
African Padauk for the drawer pull

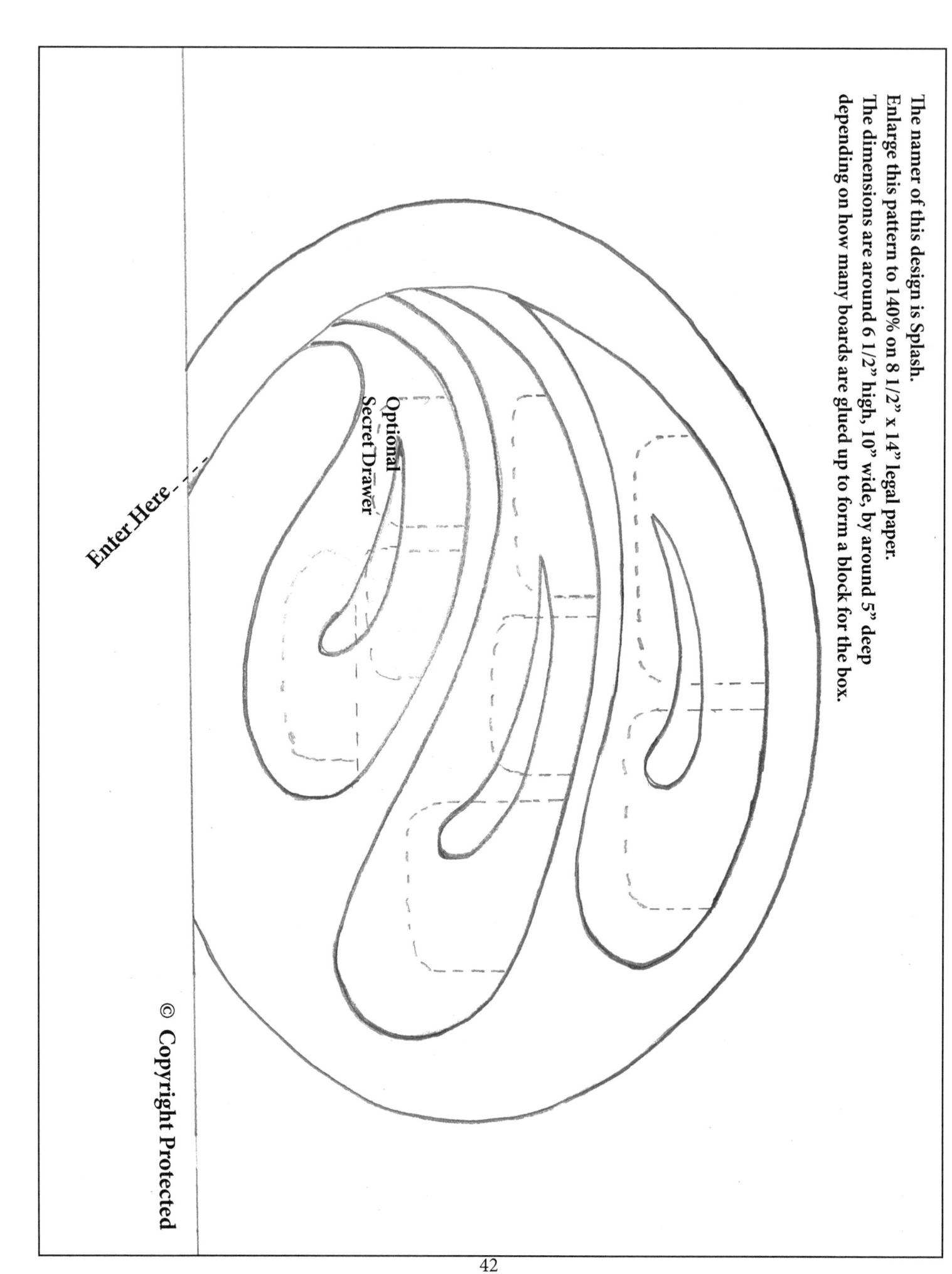

The namer of this design is Splash. Enlarge this pattern to 140% on 8 1/2" x 14" legal paper. The dimensions are around 6 1/2" high, 10" wide, by around 5" deep depending on how many boards are glued up to form a block for the box.

Enter Here

Optional Secret Drawer

© Copyright Protected

Artistry In Woodworking

Wild Bramble

This box was handcrafted with
Caribbean Walnut and
Figured Maple for the drawer pulls

44

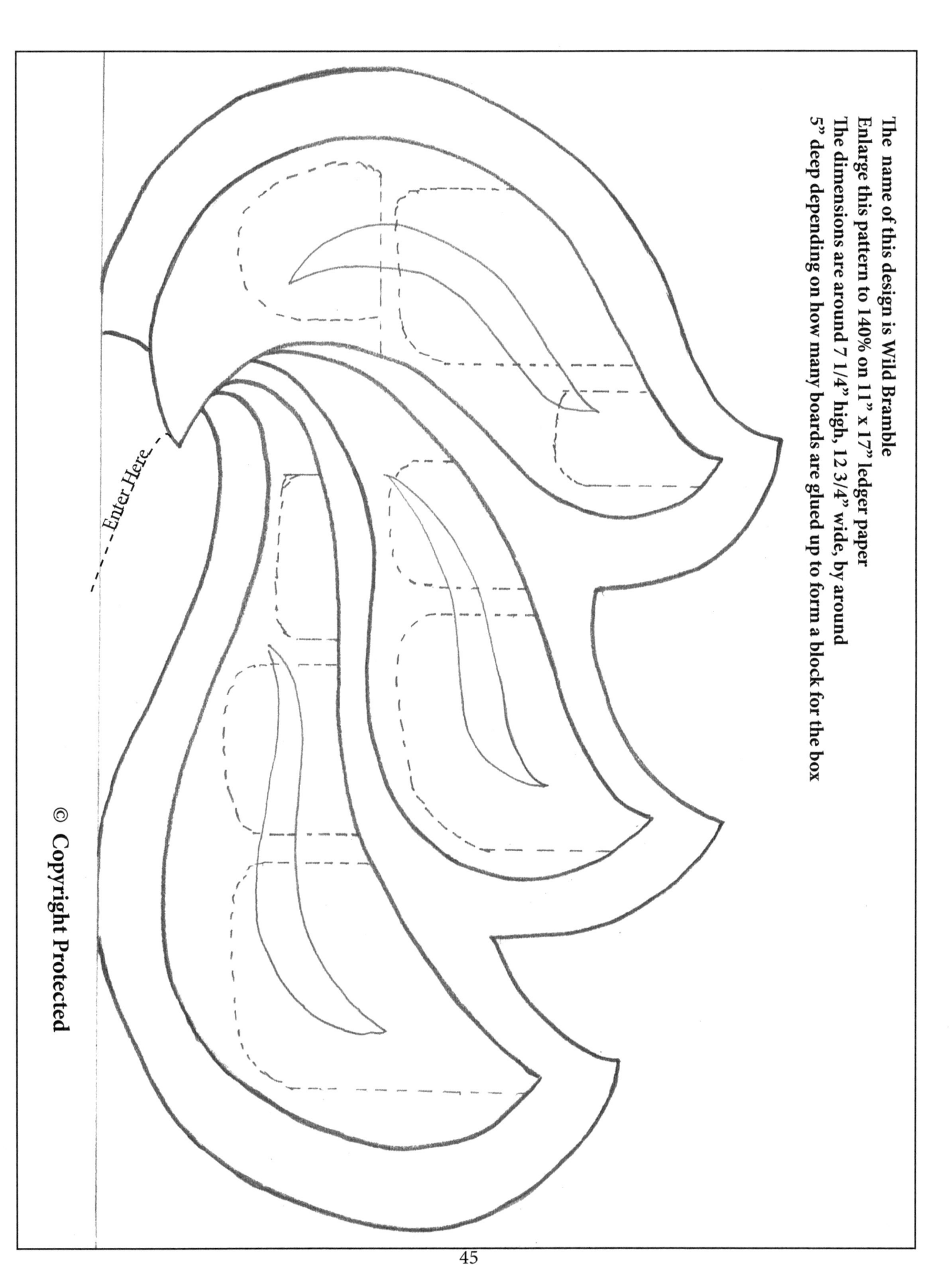

The name of this design is Wild Bramble
Enlarge this pattern to 140% on 11" x 17" ledger paper
The dimensions are around 7 1/4" high, 12 3/4" wide, by around 5" deep depending on how many boards are glued up to form a block for the box

Enter Here

© Copyright Protected

Artistry In Woodworking

Together Forever

This box was handcrafted with
Caribbean Walnut and
Figured Maple for the drawer pulls

The name of this design is Together Forever
Enlarge this patten 115% on 8 1/2" x 14" legal paper. The dimensions are 6" wide, 9 3/4" high,, by around 5" deep depending on how many boards are glued up to form a block for the box.

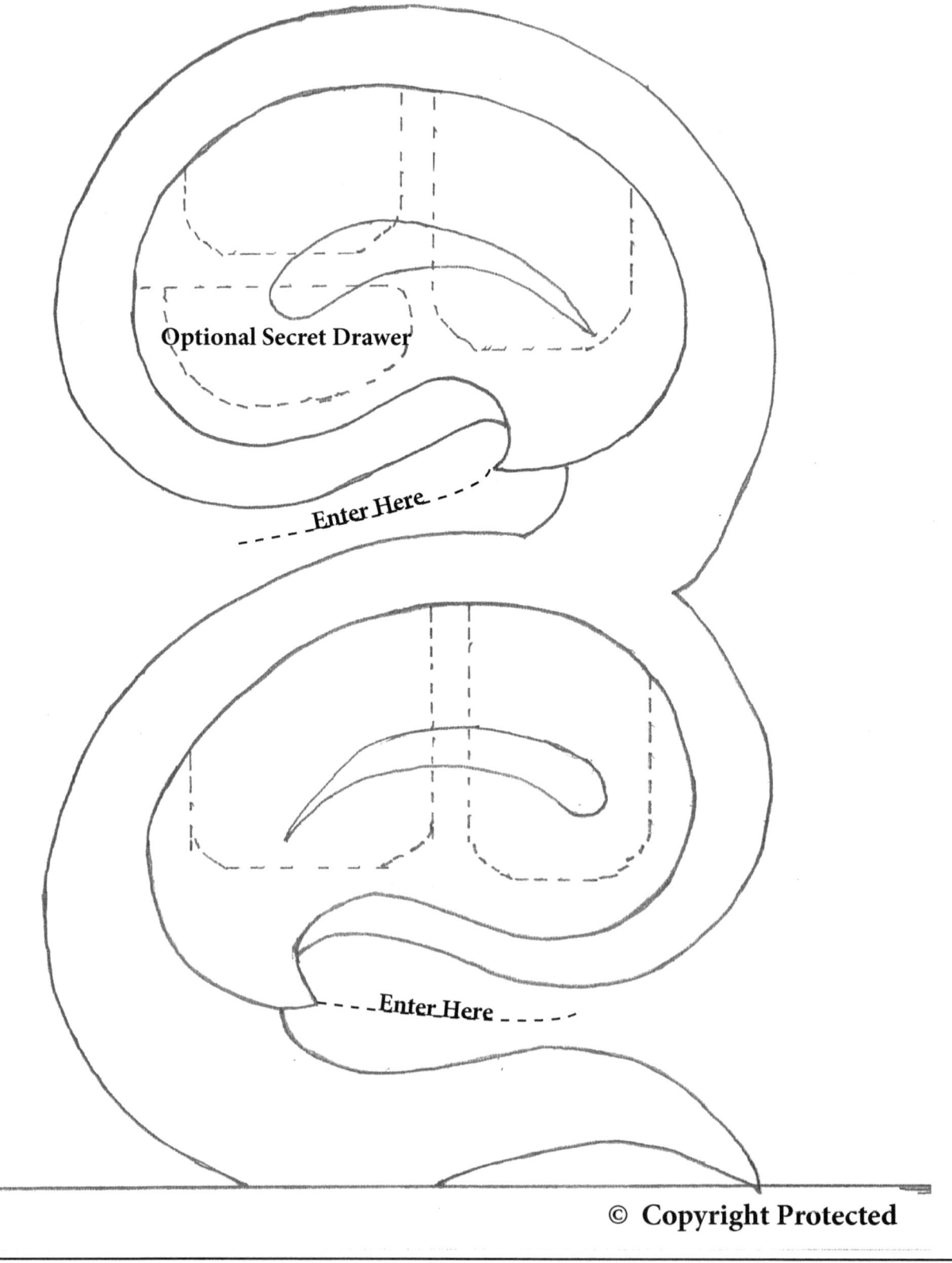

Optional Secret Drawer

Enter Here

Enter Here

© Copyright Protected

Artistry In Woodworking

Bountiful

This box was handcrafted with
African Zebrawood and
African Wenge for the drawer pulls

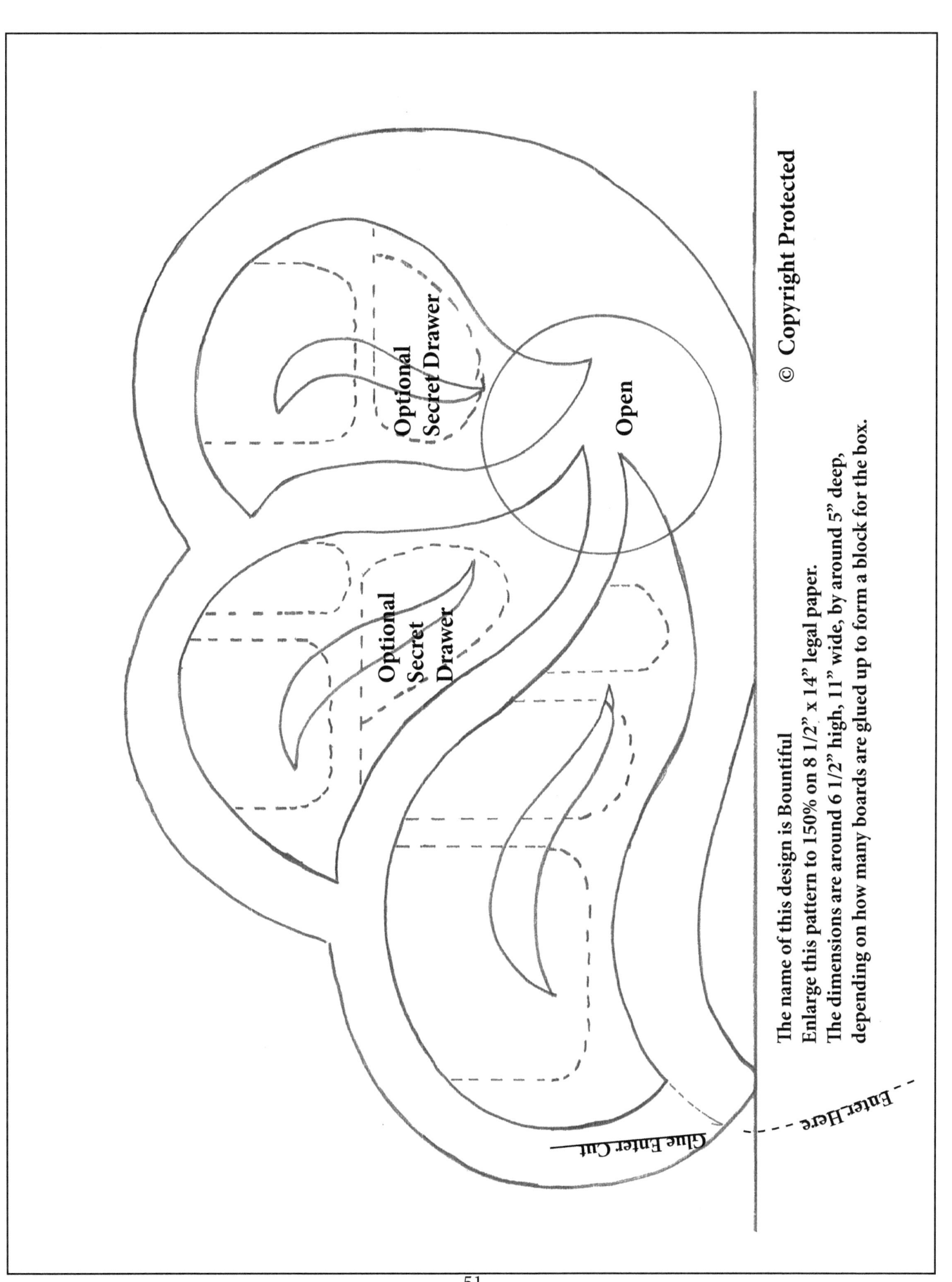

Artistry In Woodworking

Blissful Sanctum

This box was handcrafted with Caribbean Walnut and Figured Maple for the drawer pulls

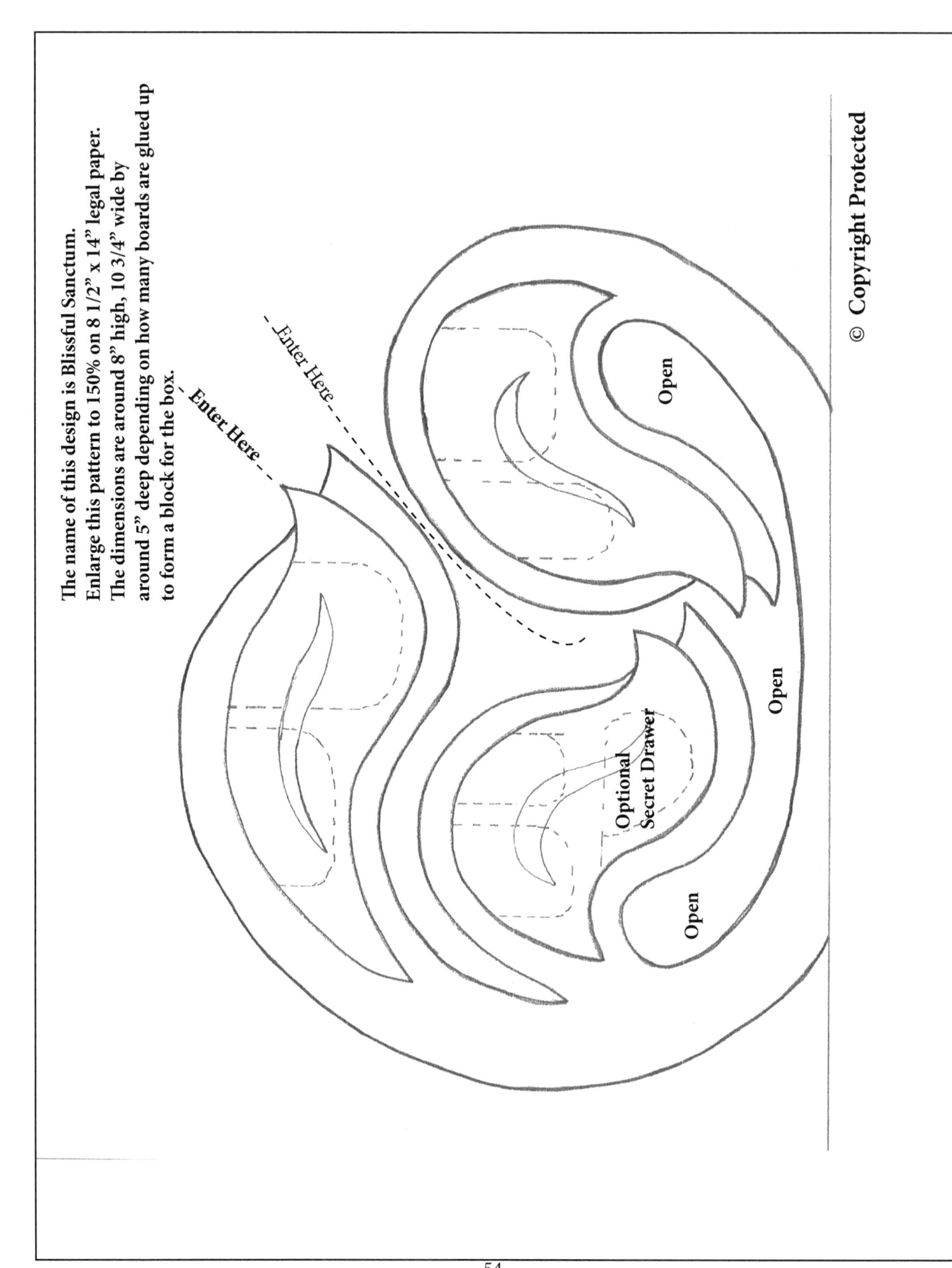

Artistry In Woodworking

Dew Drops

This box was handcrafted with
South American Katalox

The name of this pattern is Dew Drops
Enlarge this pattern to 120% on 8 1/2" x 14" legal paper.
The dimensions are around 7" high, 8 5/8" wide,
by around 5" deep depending on how many boards
are glued up to form a block for the box.

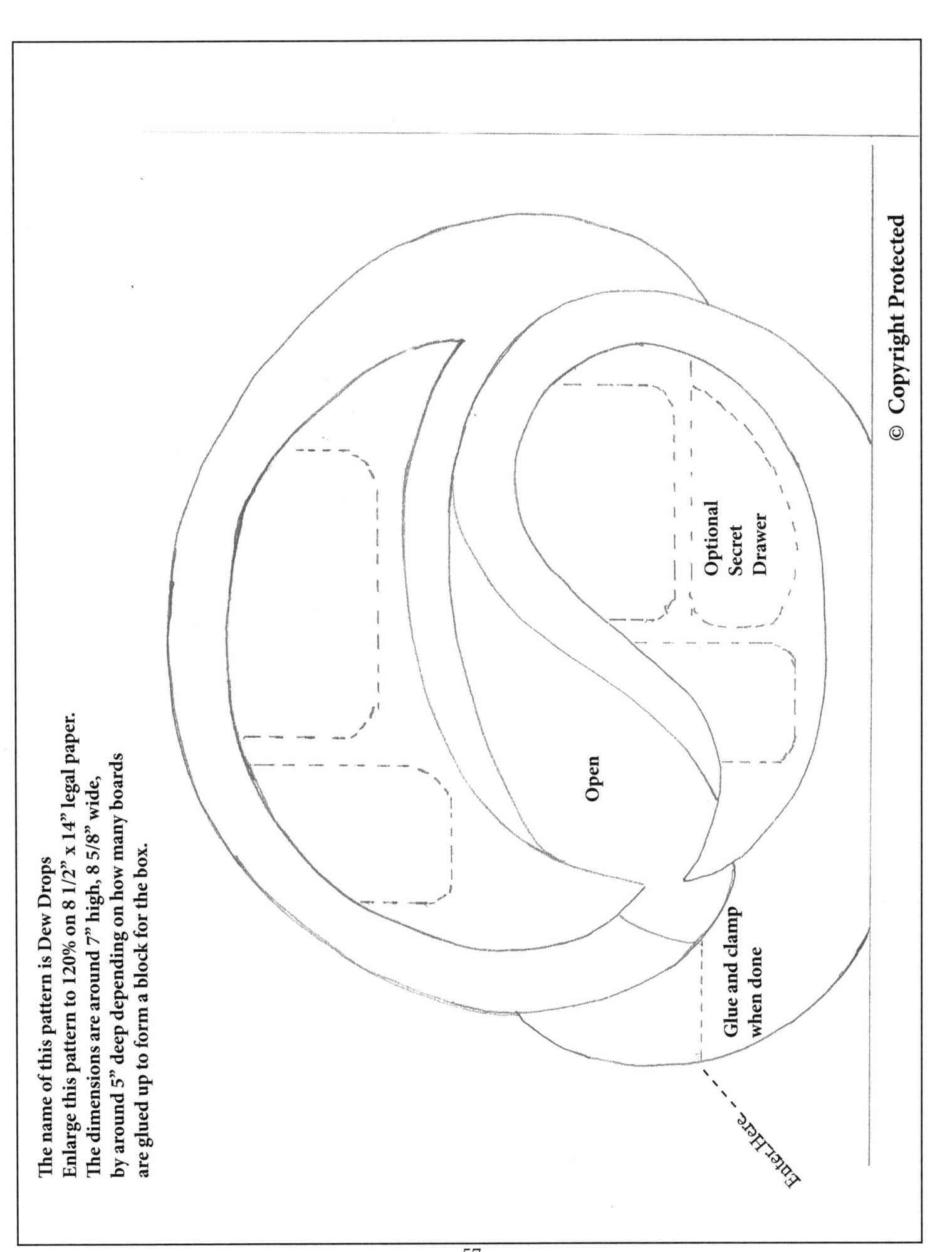

© Copyright Protected

Artistry In Woodworking

Spherical

This box was handcrafted with
South American Katalox

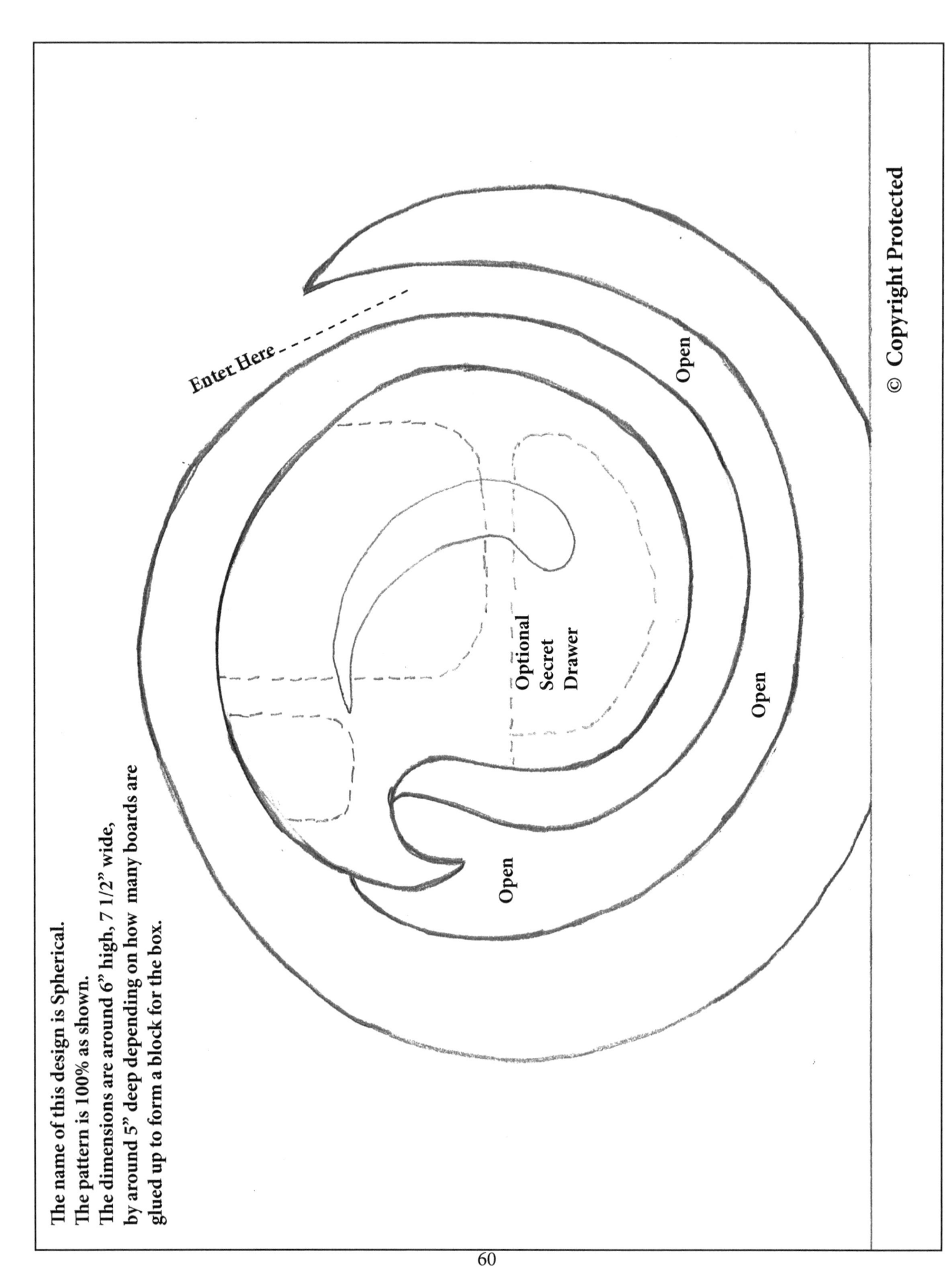

Artistry In Woodworking

Breezy Point

This box was handcrafted with
Walnut and Buckeye Burl
on the drawer front

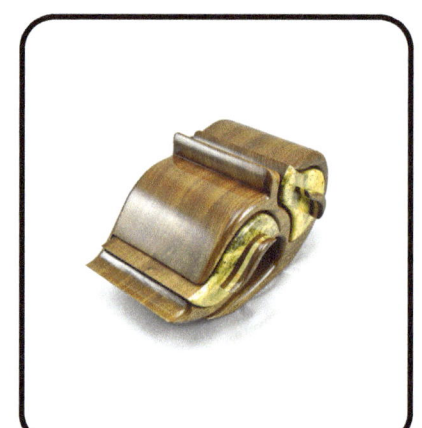

The name of this design is Breezy Point.
Enlarge this pattern to 135% on 8 1/2" x 14" legal paper.
The dimensions are around 6 1/4" high, 10 1/2" wide, by around 5" deep depending on how many boards are glued up to form a block for the box.

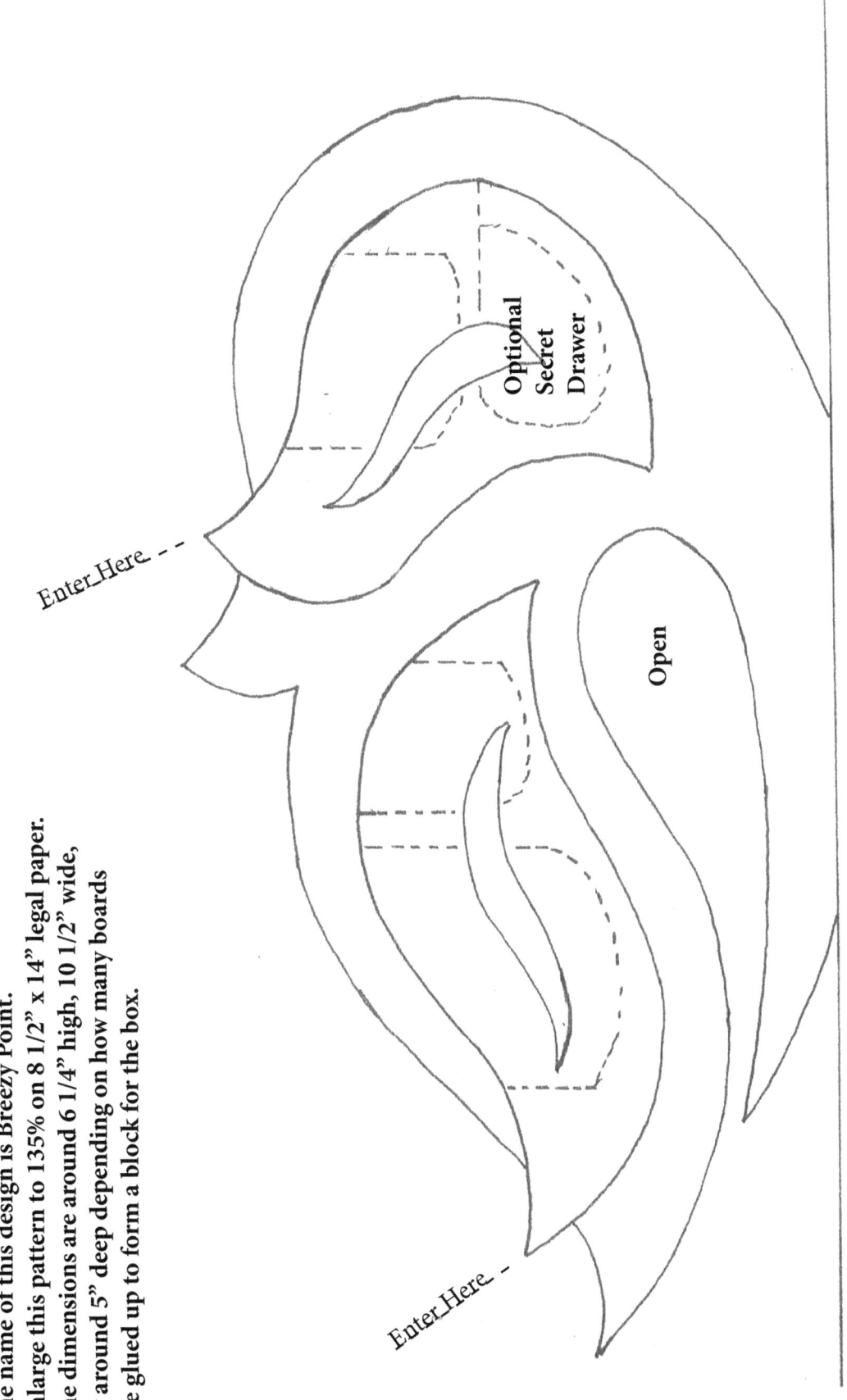

© Copyright Protected

Artistry In Woodworking

Spellbound

This box was handcrafted with African Wenge and Buckeye Burl on the drawer fronts

The Name of this design is Spellbound, Enlarge this pattern to 135% on 8 1/2" x 14" legal paper. The dimensions are around 6" high, 10 5/8" wide by around 5" deep depending on how many boards are glued up to form a block for the box.

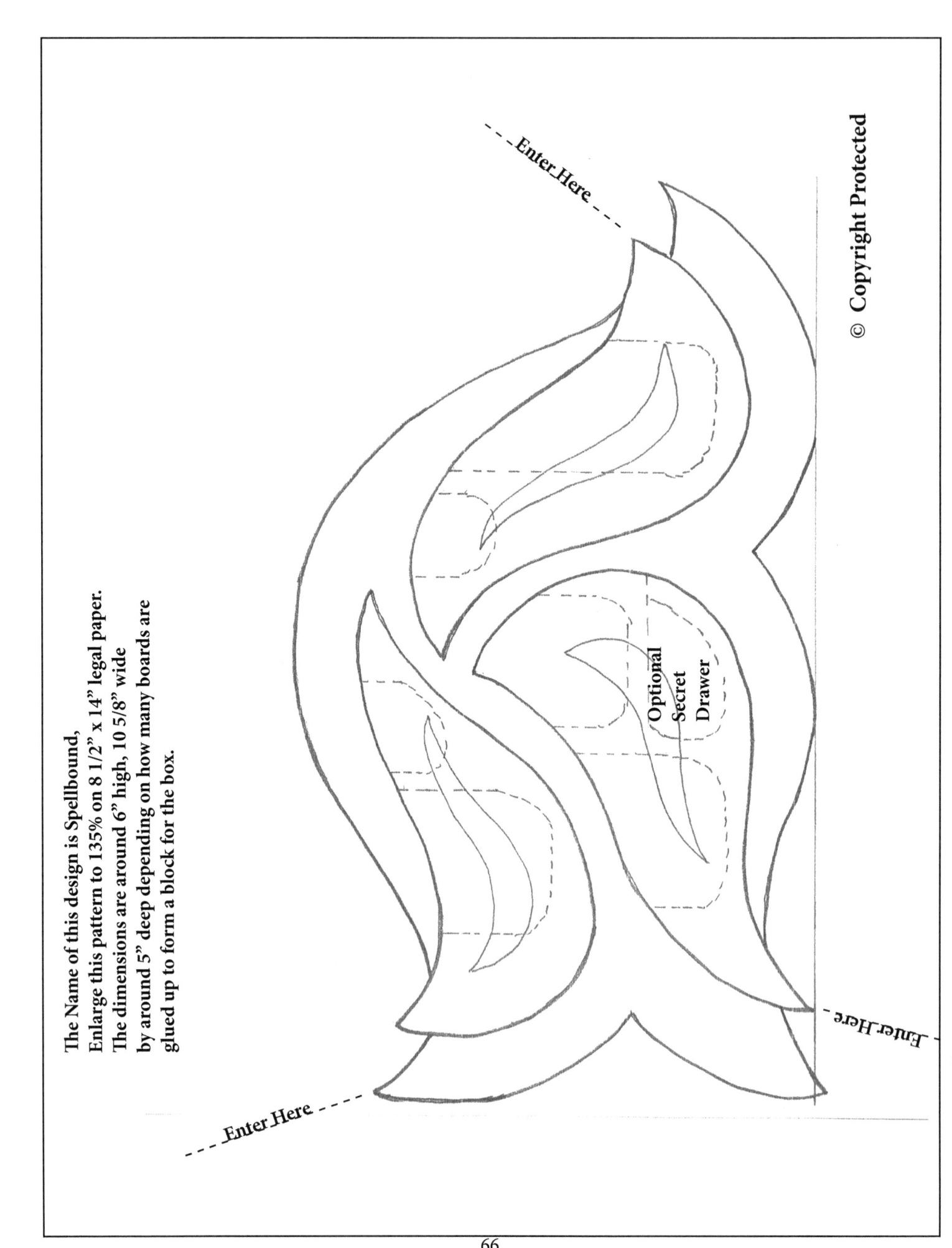

Artistry In Woodworking

Tempest

This box was handcrafted with Bolivian Picana and Figured Maple for the drawer pulls

The name of this design is Tempest
Enlarge this pattern to 130% on 8 1/2" x 14" legal paper.
The dimensions are around 6 1/2" high, 11 1/4" wide,
by around 5" deep, depending on how many boards
are glued up to form a block for the box.

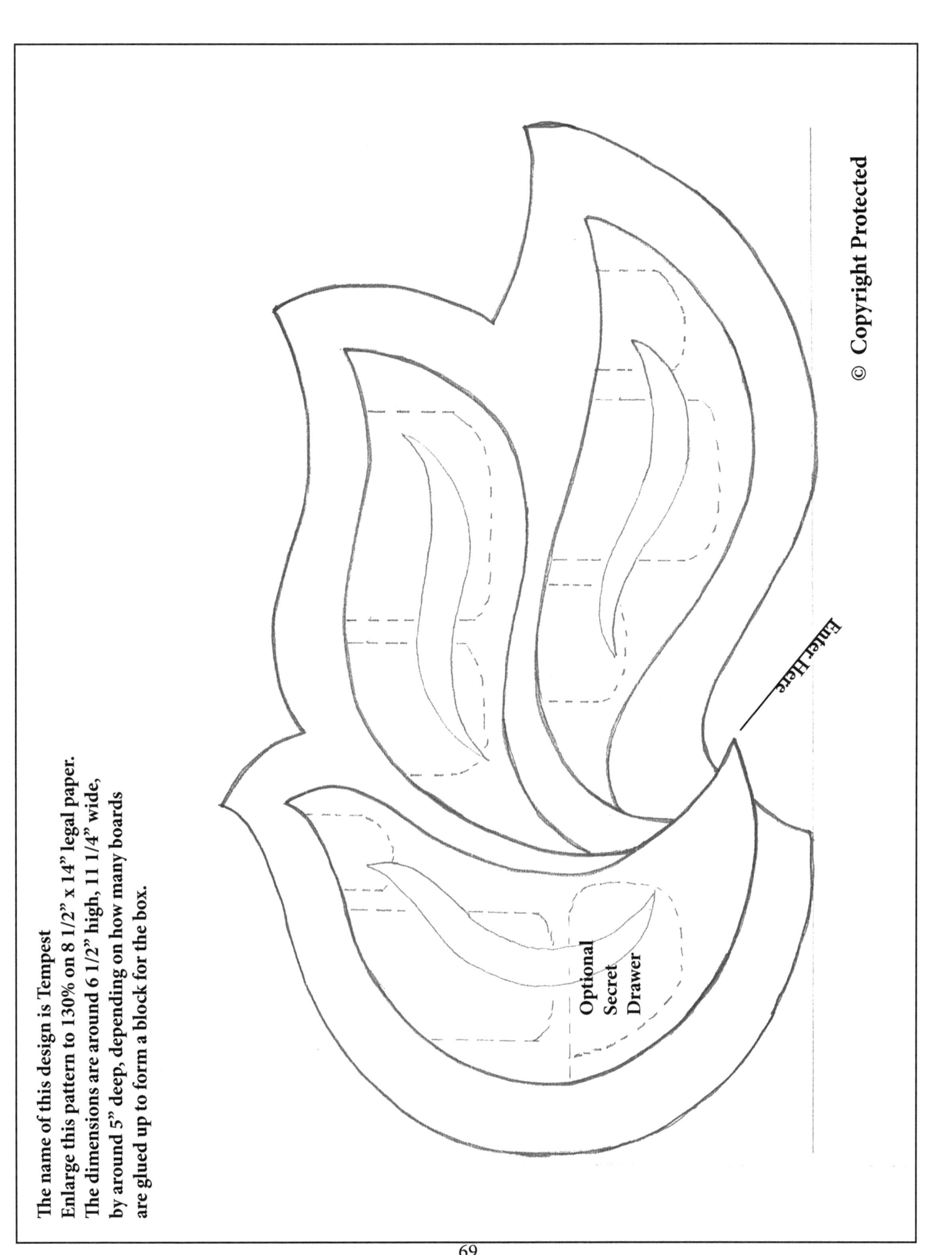

© Copyright Protected

Enter Here

Optional Secret Drawer

Artistry In Woodworking

Twilight

**This box was handcrafted with
Caribbean Rosewood
and Figured Maple for the drawer pulls**

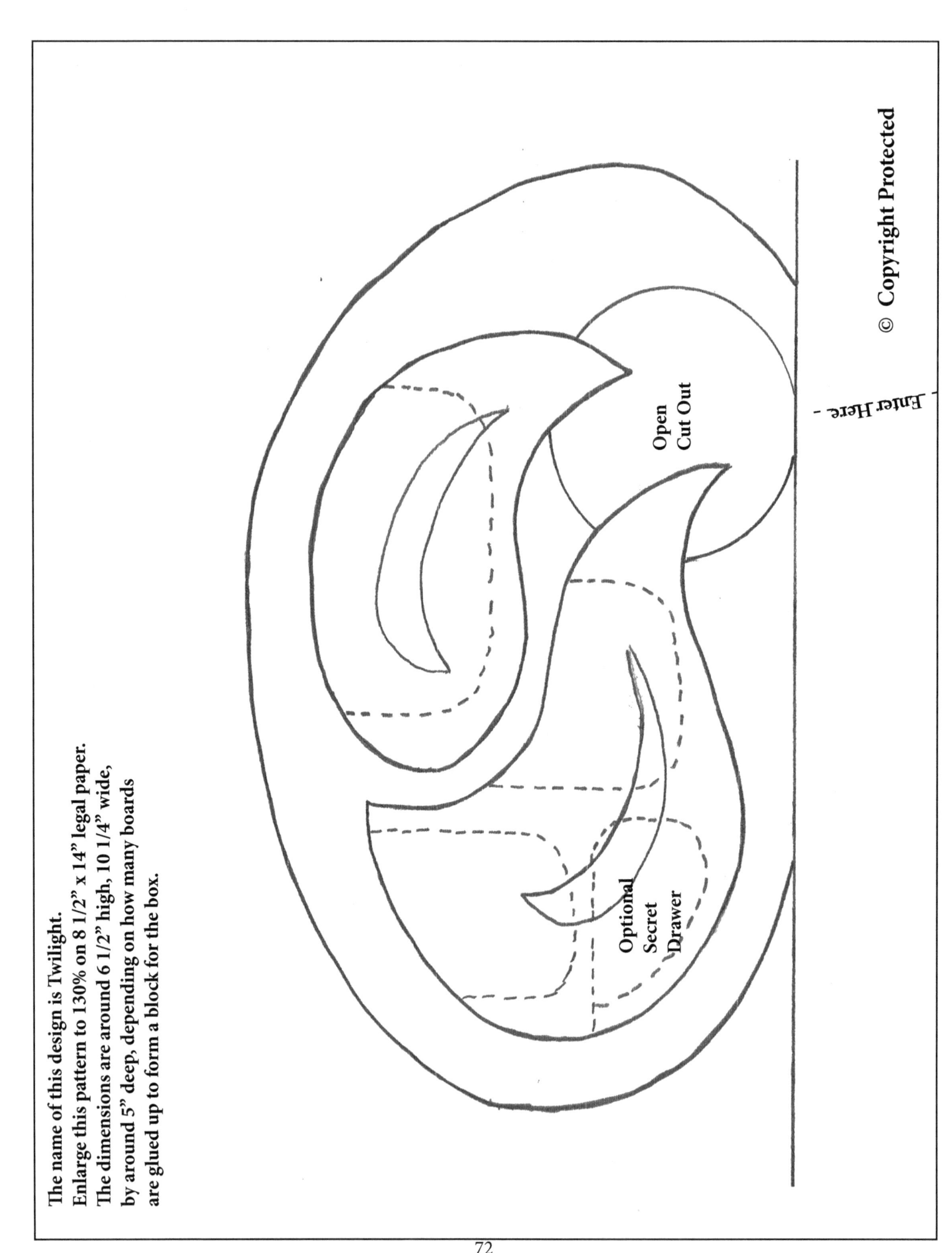

Artistry In Woodworking

Cascade

This box was handcrafted with
Caribbean Rosewood
and Figured Maple for the drawer pulls

The name of this design is Cascade.
Enlarge this pattern to 150% on 11" x 17" ledger paper. The dimensions are around 6 1/4" high, 12 3/4" wide, by around 5" deep, depending on how many boards are glued up to form a block for the box.

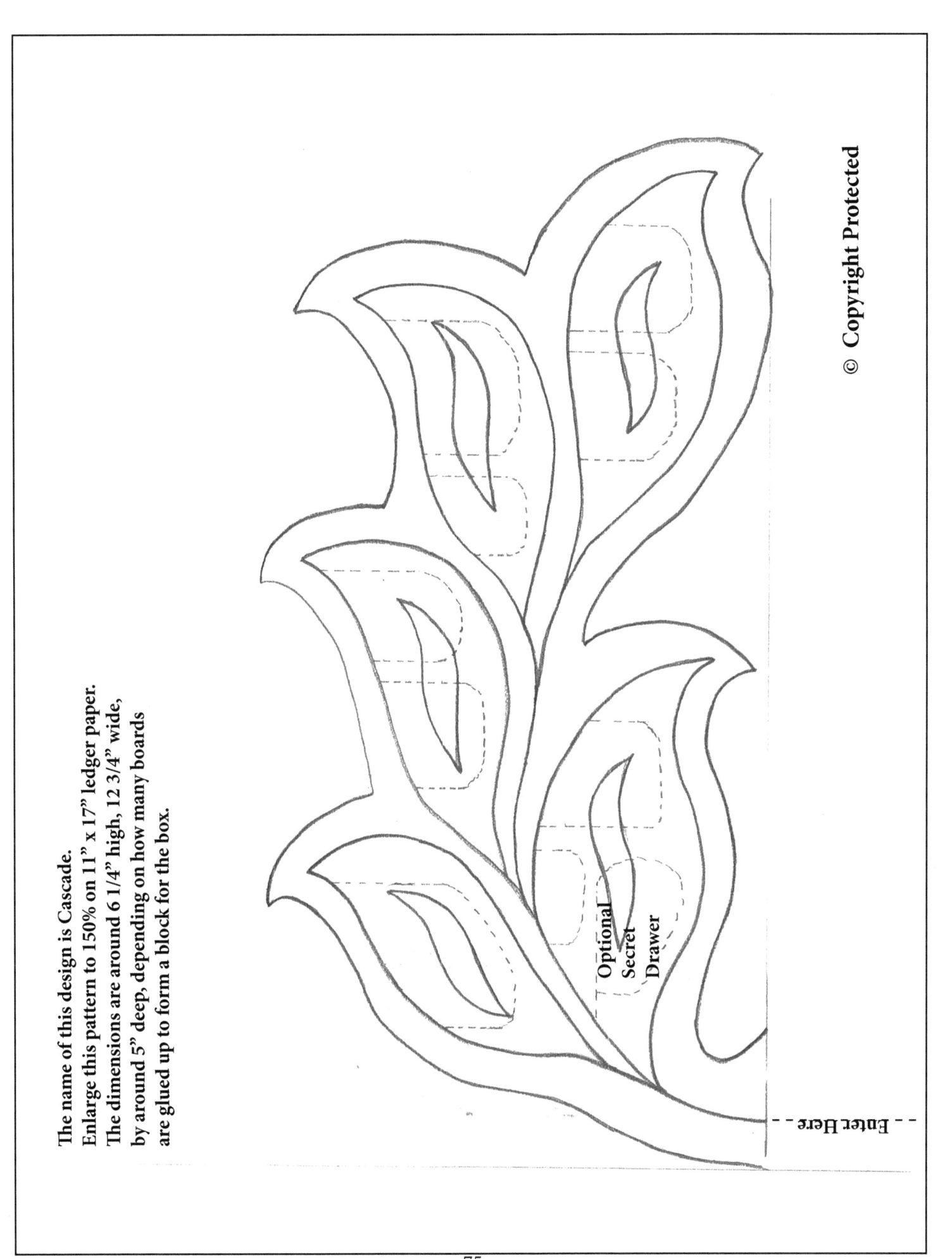

© Copyright Protected

Optional Secret Drawer

- - - Enter Here

Artistry In Woodworking

Sea Shell

This box was handcrafted with
Caribbean Rosewood
and Figured Maple for the drawer pulls

The name of this design is Sea Shell. Enlarge this pattern on 8 1/2" x 14" legal paper. The dimensions are around 5 1/2" High, 10" wide, by around 5" deep depending on how many boards are glued up to form a block for the box.

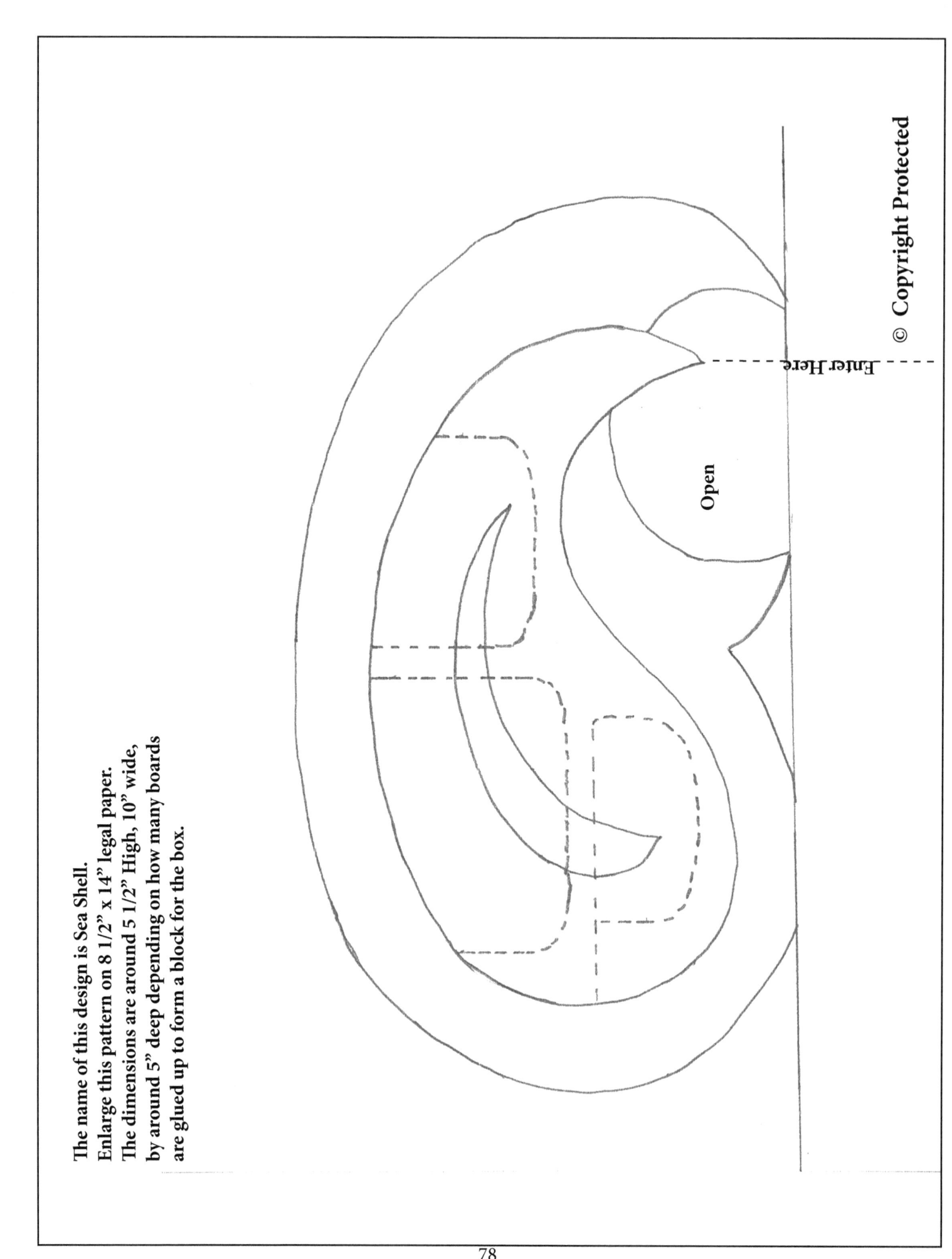

Artistry In Woodworking

Summer Tree

This box was handcrafted with African Wenge and Buckeye Burl on the drawer fronts

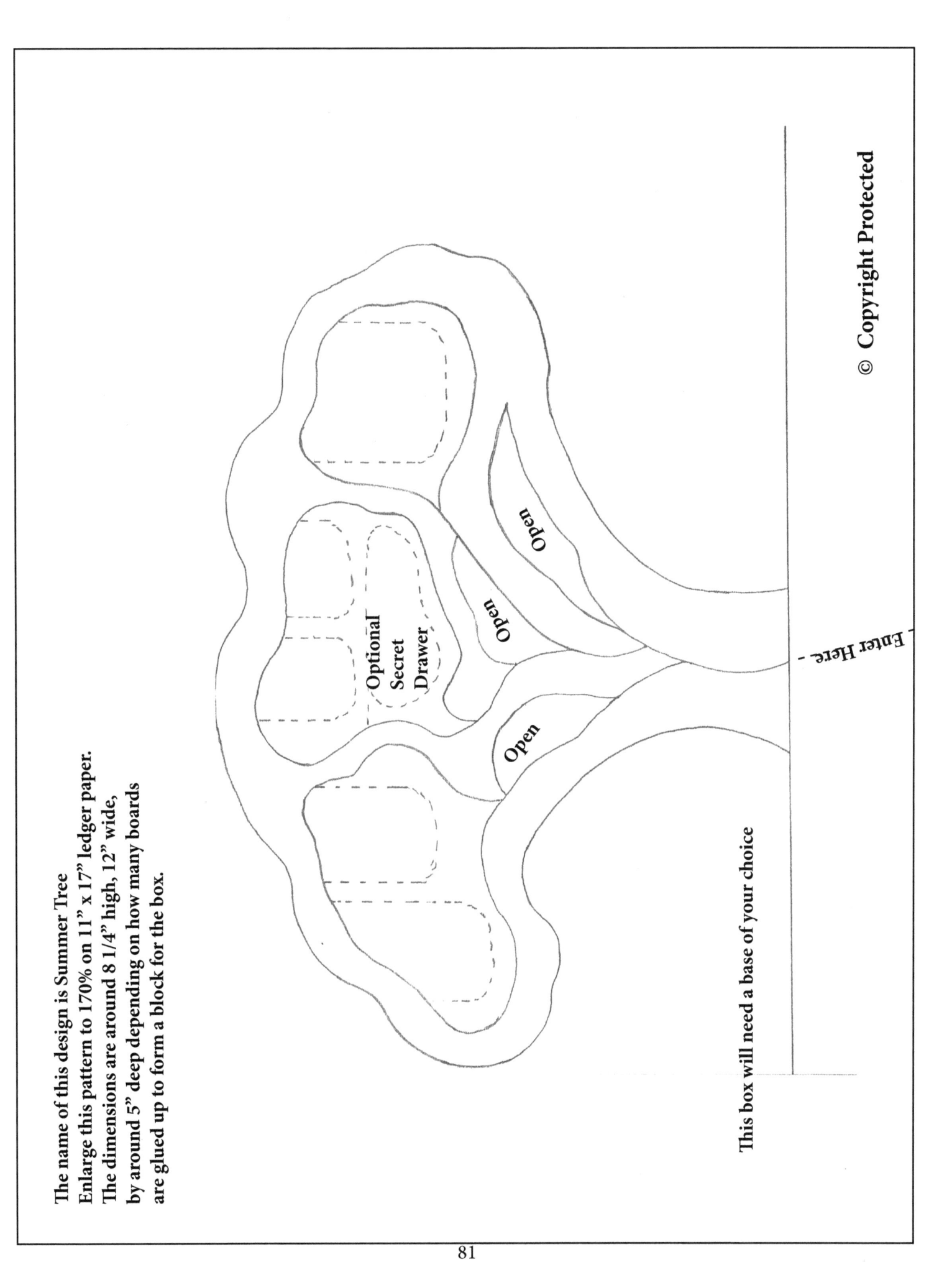

The name of this design is Summer Tree
Enlarge this pattern to 170% on 11" x 17" ledger paper.
The dimensions are around 8 1/4" high, 12" wide,
by around 5" deep depending on how many boards
are glued up to form a block for the box.

Optional Secret Drawer

Open
Open
Open

Enter Here

This box will need a base of your choice

© Copyright Protected

Artistry In Woodworking

Tea Pot

This box was handcrafted with African Kiaat and African Padauk for the drawer pull

Enter Here

Optional Secret Drawer

Open

The name of this design is Tea Pot
Enlarge this pattern to 110% on 8 1/2" x 11" letter paper.
The dimensions are around 5 3/4" high, 8 1/2" wide, by around 5" deep, depending on how many boards are glued up to form a block for the box.

© Copyright Protected

Artistry In Woodworking

Bristly Virgin

This box was handcrafted with South American Bloodwood and Figured Maple for the drawer pulls

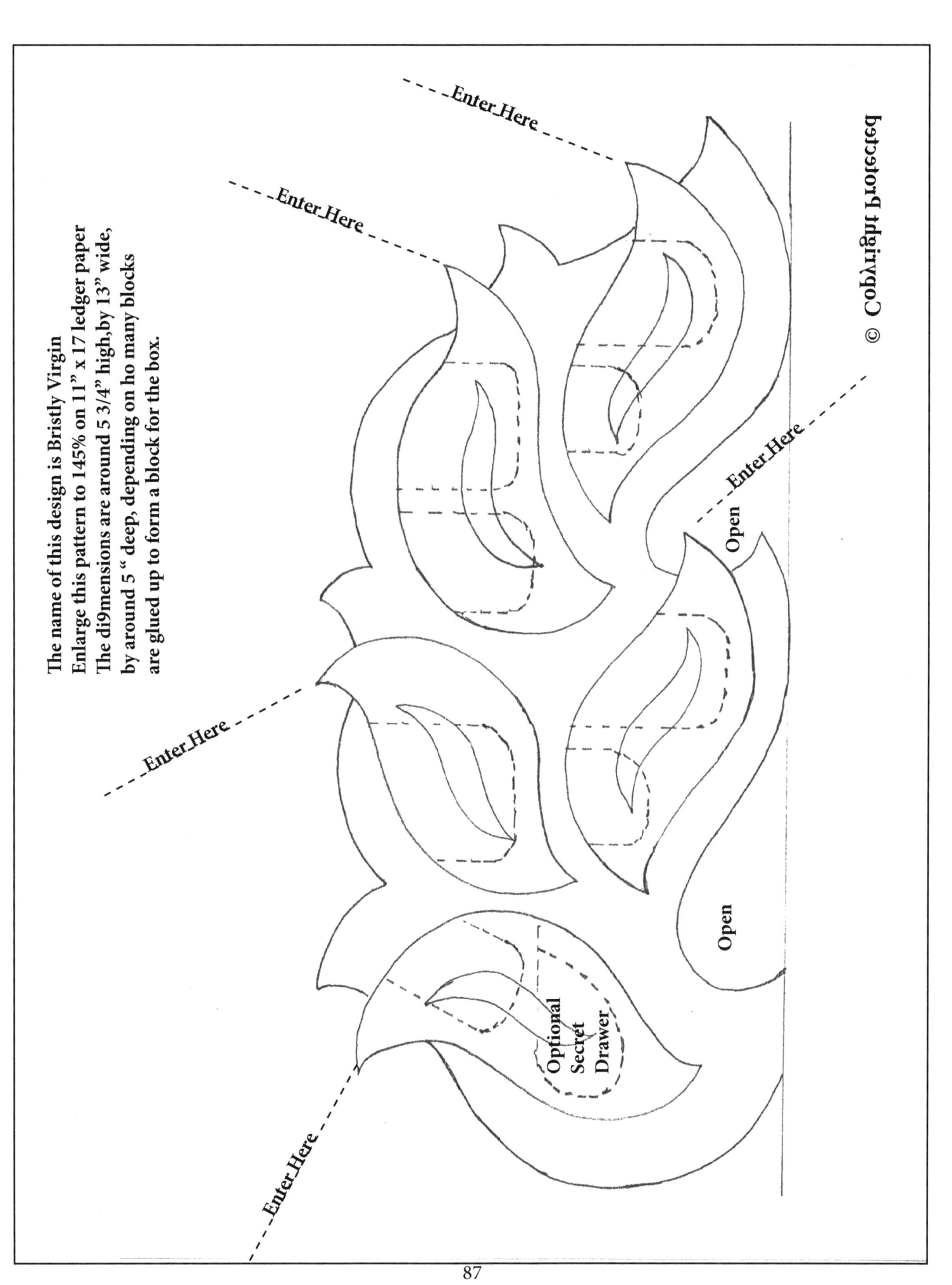

Artistry In Woodworking

Enchanted

This box was handcrafted with
Walnut and Buckeye Burl
on the drawer fronts

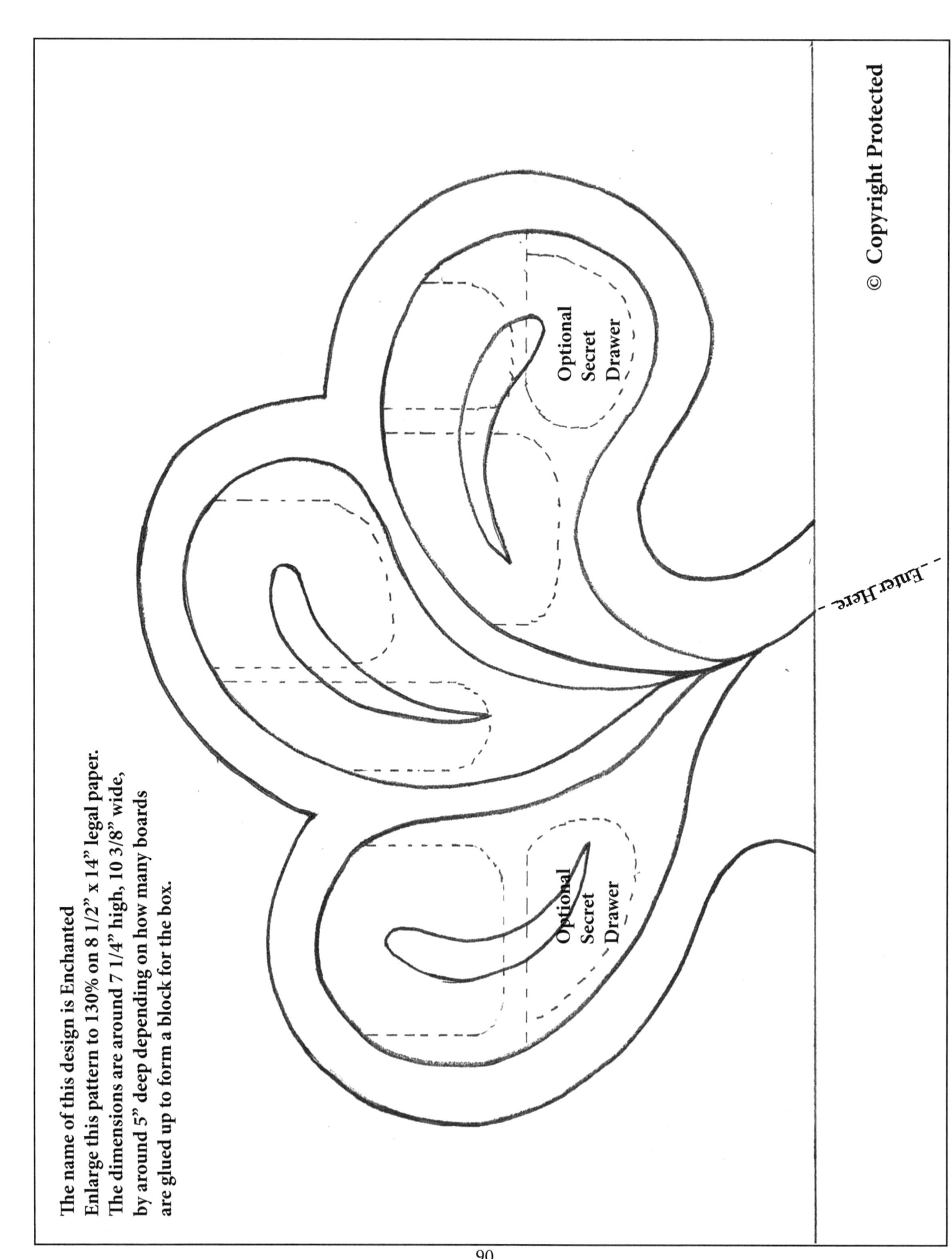

Artistry In Woodworking

Windblown

This box was handcrafted with African Kiaat and African Padauk for the drawer pulls

The name of this design is Windblown
Enlarge this pattern to 145% on 11" x 14" ledger paper.
The dimensions are around 10 3/4" high, 9" wide,
by around 5" deep depending on how many boards
are glued up to form a block for the box.

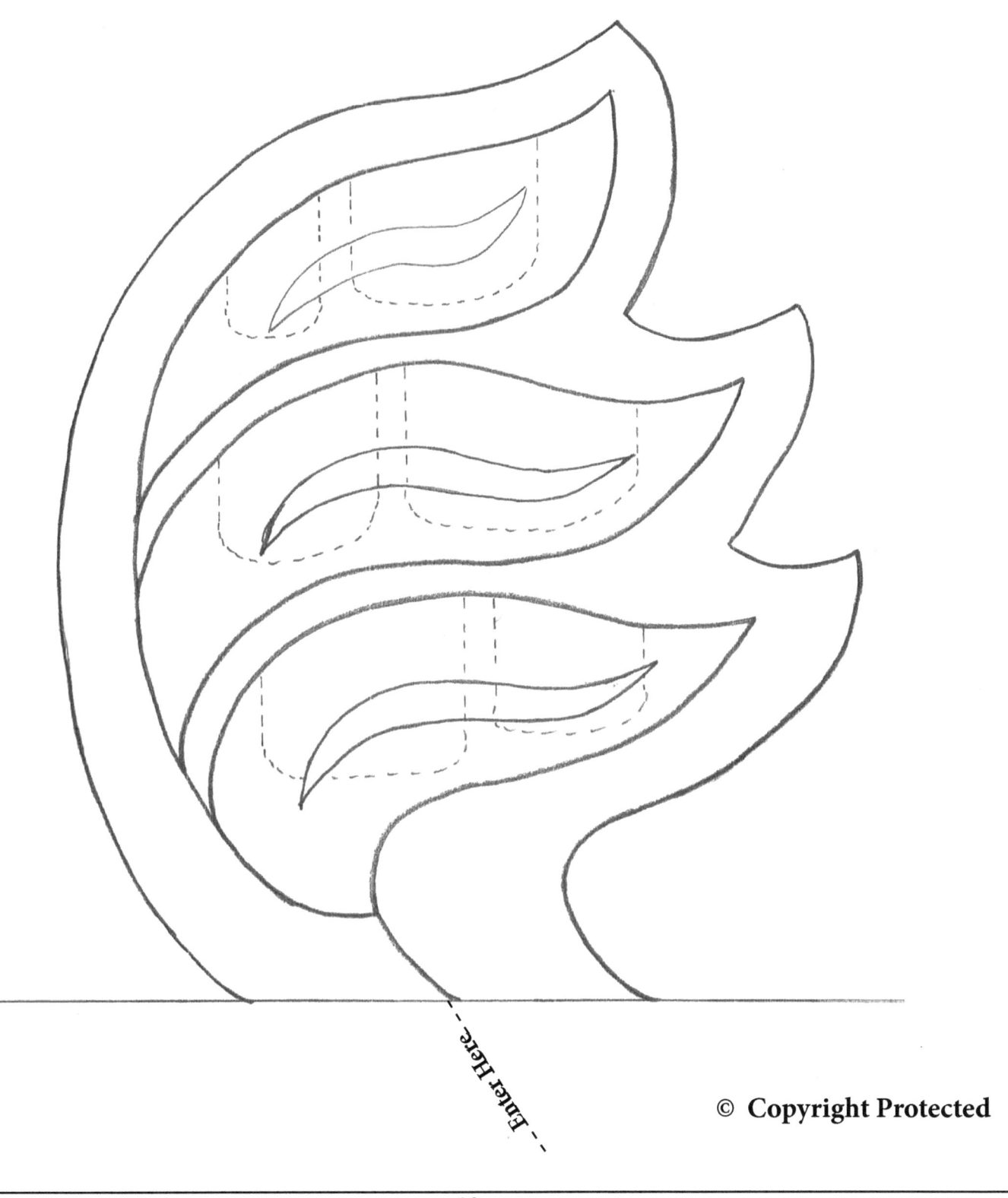

© Copyright Protected

Artistry In Woodworking

The Phantom

This box was handcrafted with
African Wenge and Buckeye Burl
on the drawer fronts

The name of this design is The Phantom
Enlarge this pattern to 120% on 8 1/2" x 14" legal paper.
The dimensions are around 4 1/2" high, 10" wide,
by around 5" deep depending on how many boards are
glued up to form a block for the box.

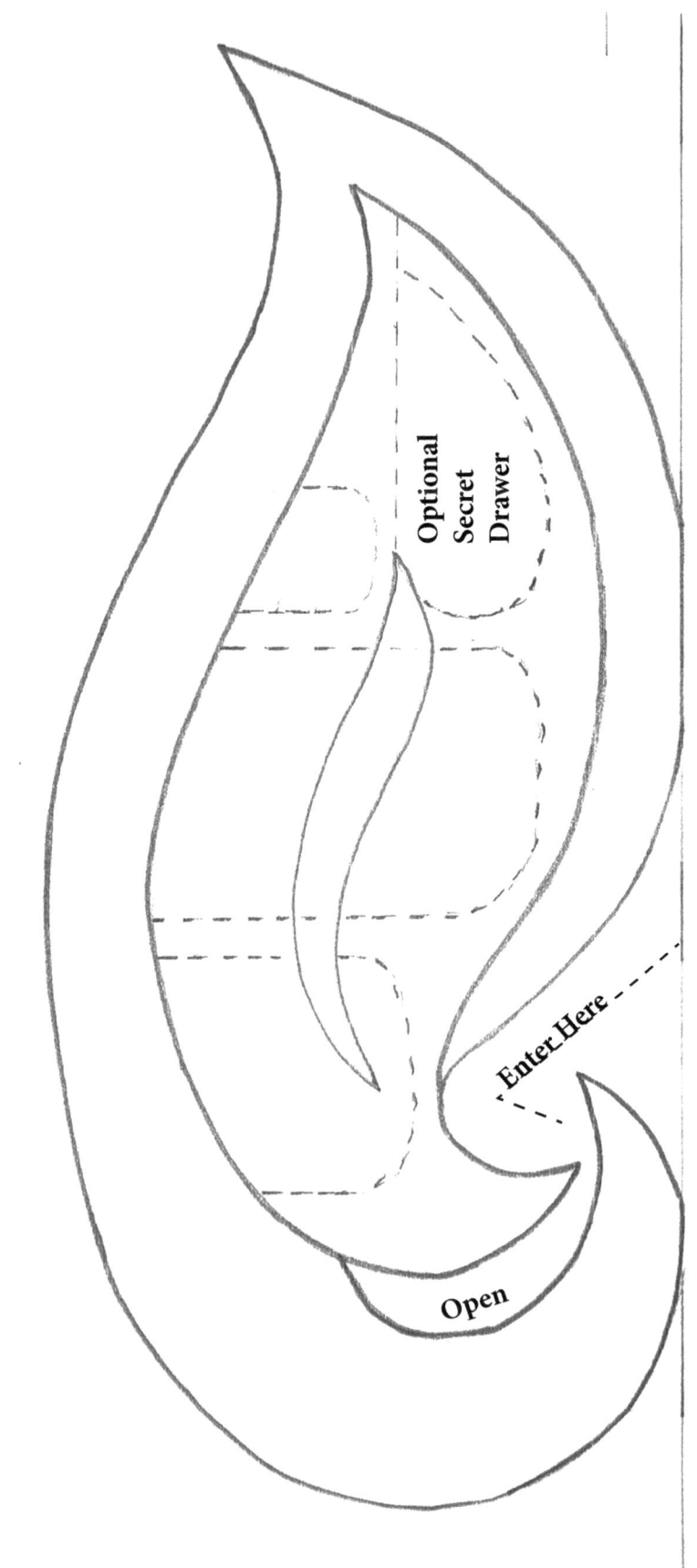

Optional Secret Drawer

Enter Here

Open

© Copyright Protected

Artistry In Woodworking

Majestic Tree

This box was handcrafted with Ambrosia Maple with Brazilian Tigerwood for the drawer pulls

The name of this design is Majestic Tree
Enlarge this pattern to 150% on 11" x 17" ledger paper.
The dimensions are around 7" high x 11" wide,
by around 5" deep depending on how many boards
are glued up to form a block for the box.

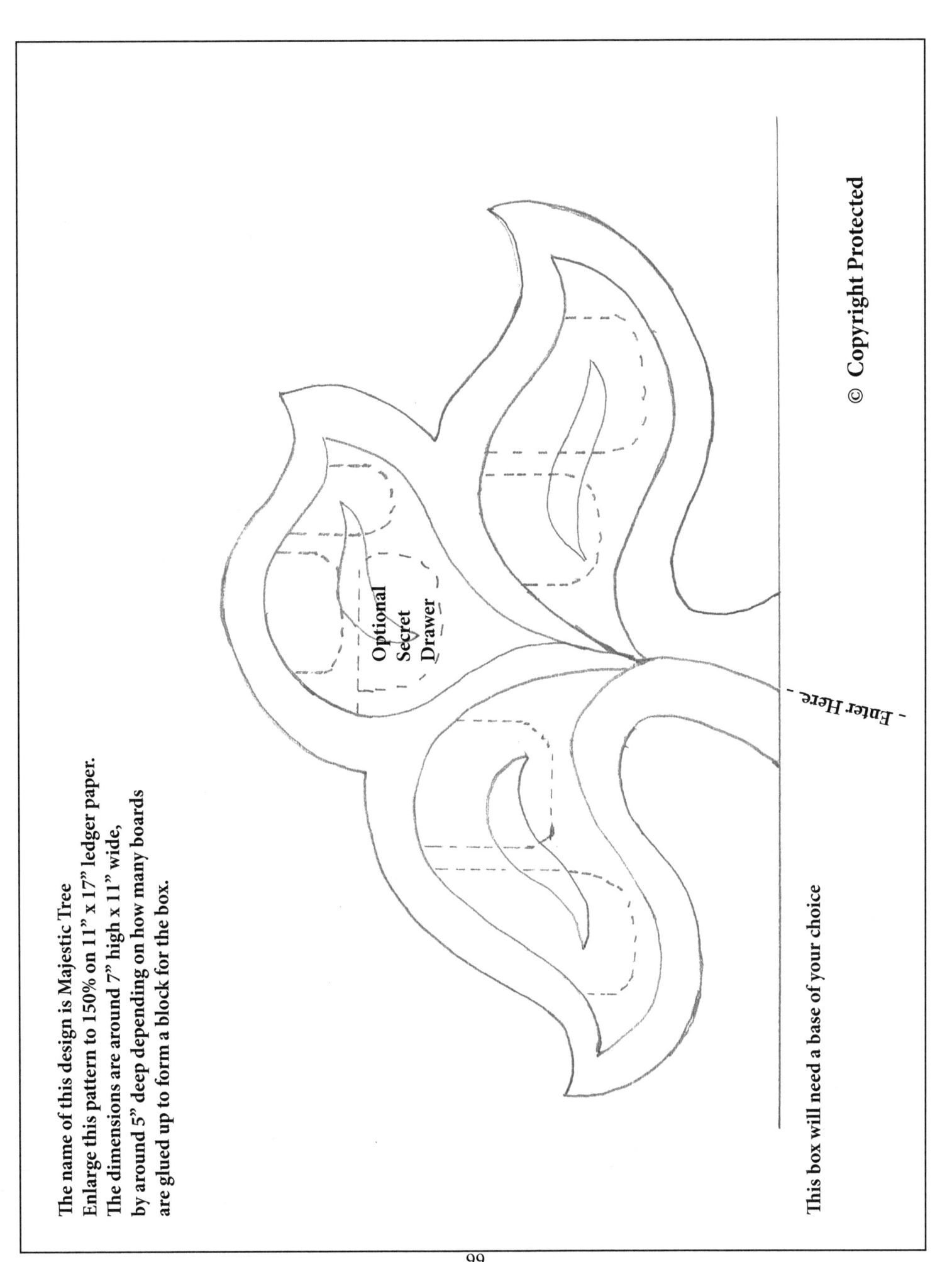

Optional Secret Drawer

Enter Here

This box will need a base of your choice

© Copyright Protected

Artistry In Woodworking

Serengeti III

This box was handcrafted with African Black Limba and African Wenge for the drawer pulls

The name of this design is Serengeti III
Enlarge this pattern to 150% on 11" x 17" ledger paper.
The dimensions are around 8" high, 11 1/2" wide,
by around 5" deep, depending on how many boards
are glued up to form a block for the box.
This box will need a base of your choice.

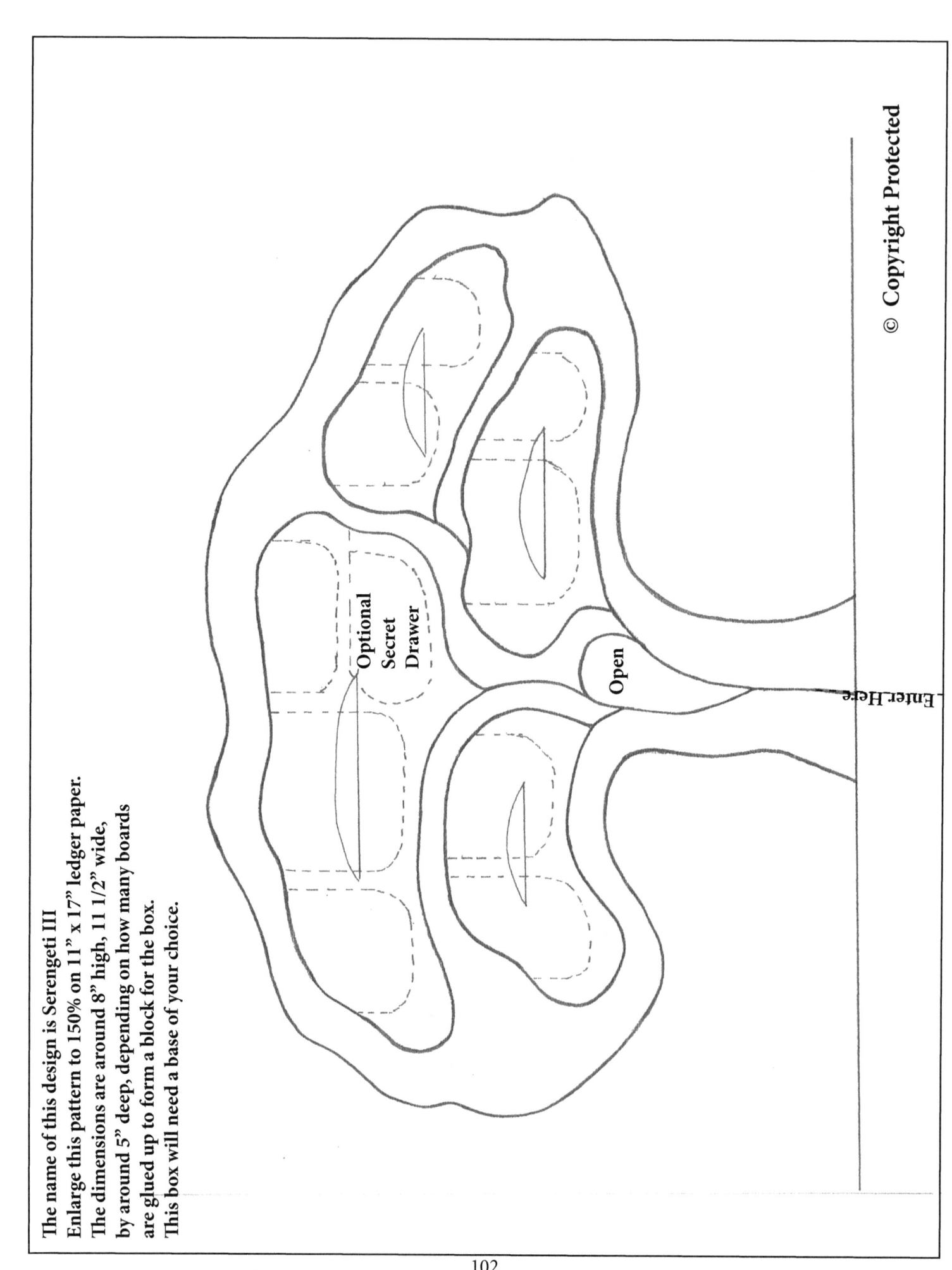

Artistry In Woodworking

Serengeti IV

This box was handcrafted with
Walnut and Buckeye Burl
on the drawer fronts

The name of this design is Serengeti IV
Enlarge this pattern to 140 % on 11 x 17" ledger paper
The dimensions are around 7 3/4" high, 12" wide,
by around 5" deep, depending on how many
boards are glued up to form a block for the box.
You will need a base of your choice for this box,

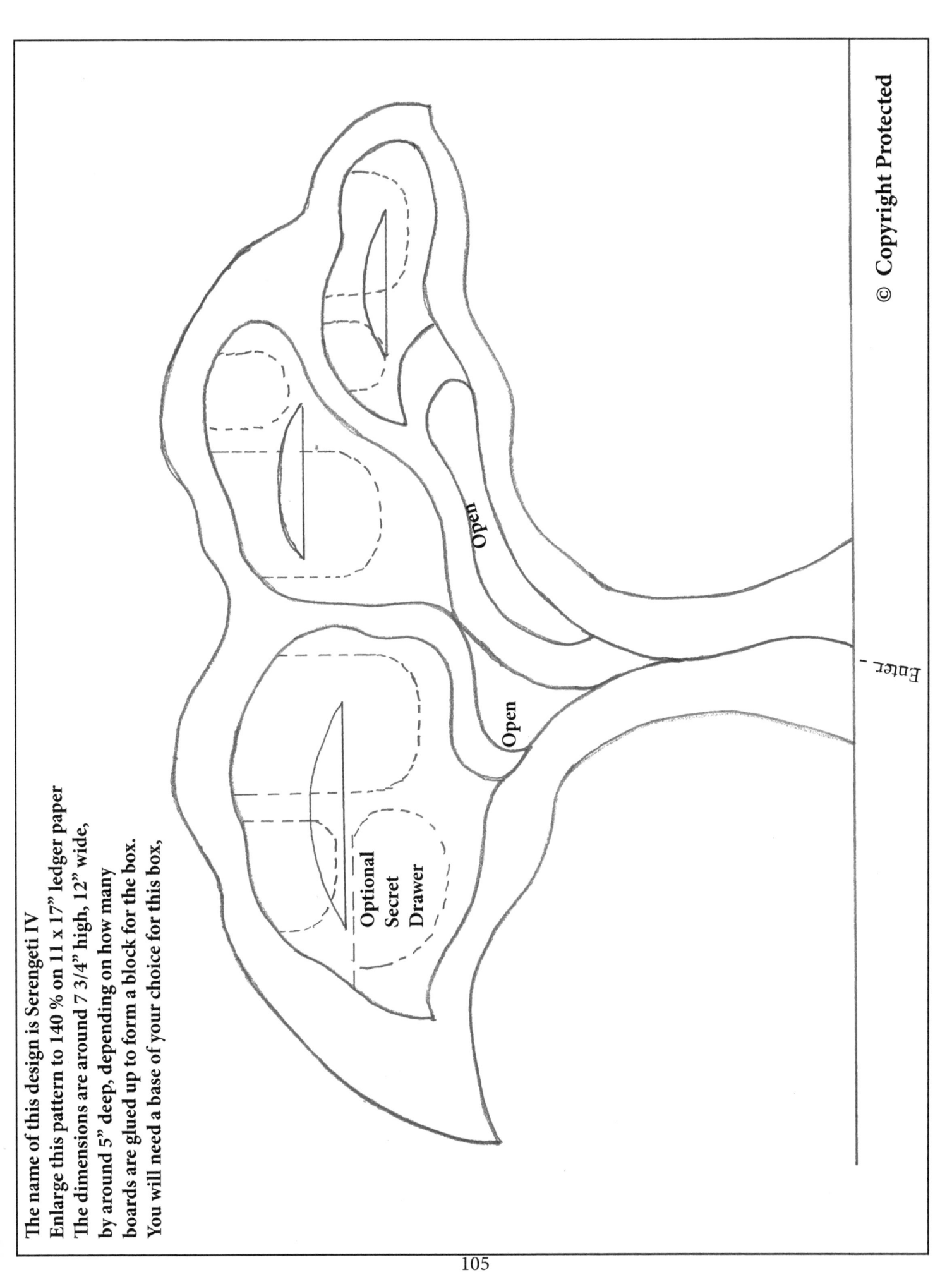

Artistry In Woodworking

Magnum

This box was handcrafted with African Padauk and Figured Maple for the drawer pulls

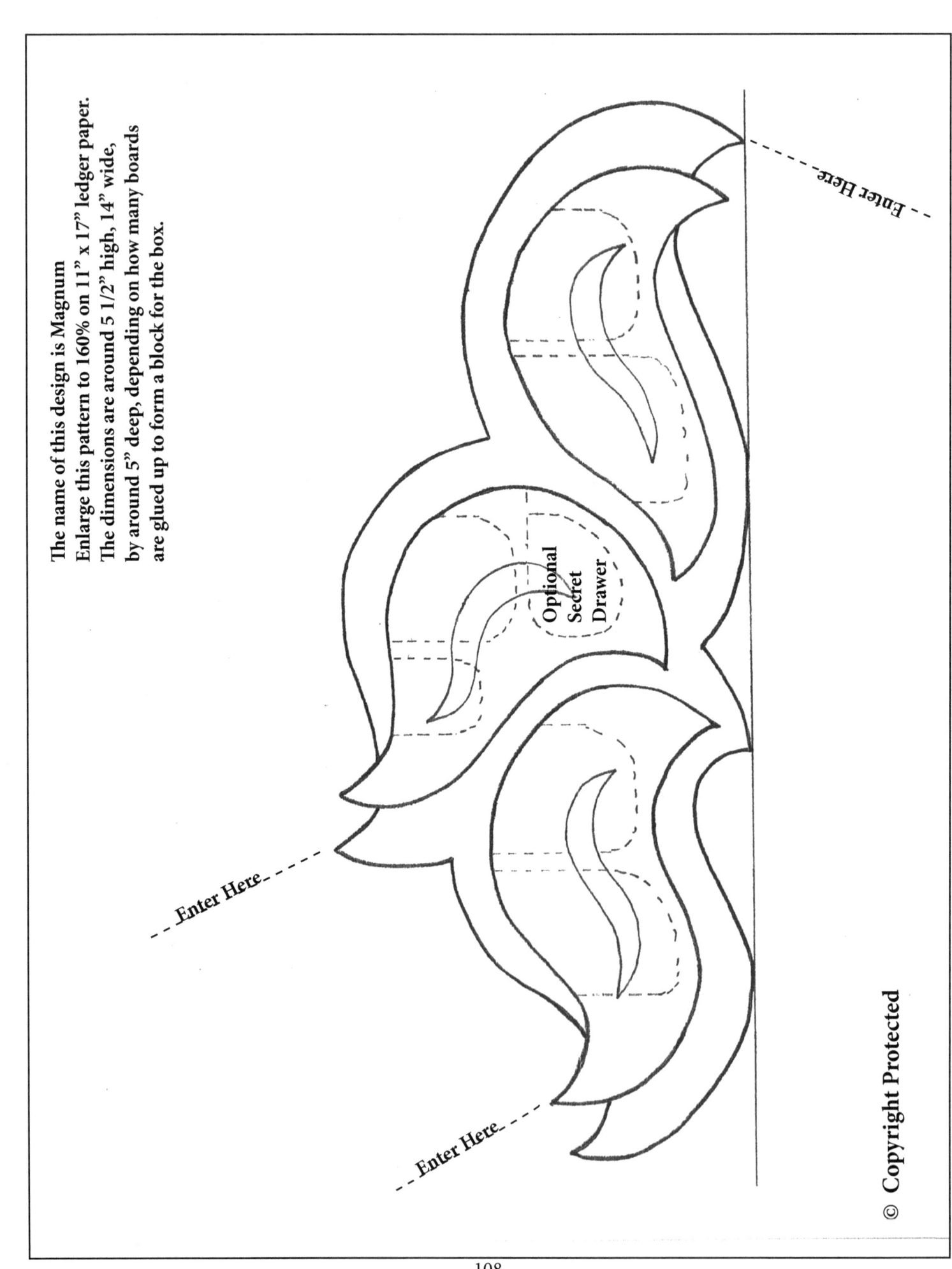

The name of this design is Magnum
Enlarge this pattern to 160% on 11" x 17" ledger paper. The dimensions are around 5 1/2" high, 14" wide, by around 5" deep, depending on how many boards are glued up to form a block for the box.

Optional Secret Drawer

Enter Here

© Copyright Protected

Artistry In Woodworking

Lovers

This box was handcrafted with African Padauk and Figured Maple for the drawer pulls

The name of this design is Lovers
Enlarge this pattern 150% on 8 1/2" x 14" legal paper.
The dimensions are around 5 1/2" high, 10 1/4" wide, by around 5" deep, depending on how many boards are glued up to form a block for the box.

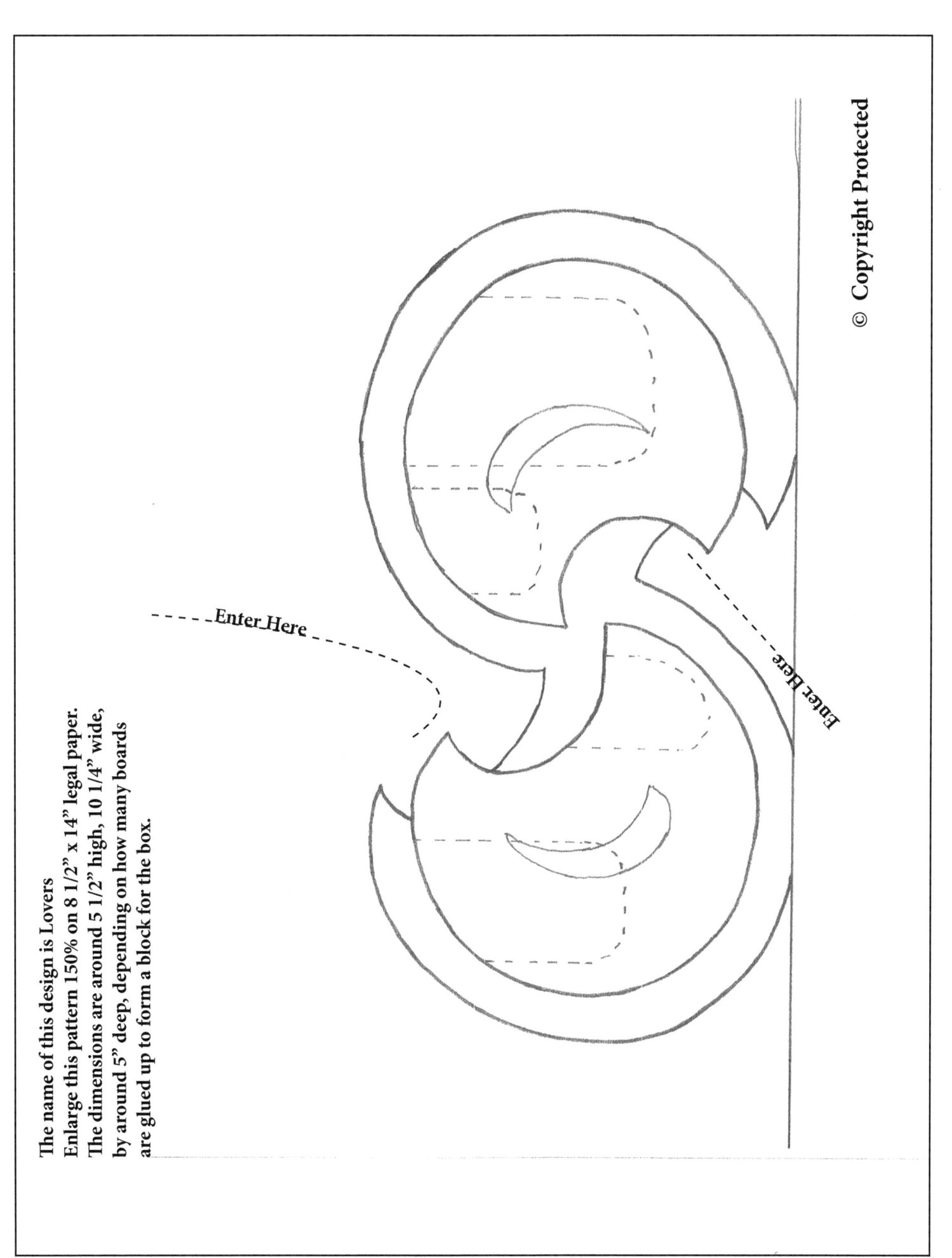

© Copyright Protected

Artistry In Woodworking

Winter Berries

This box was handcrafted with
Spalted Hack Berry and African Ebony
for the drawer pulls

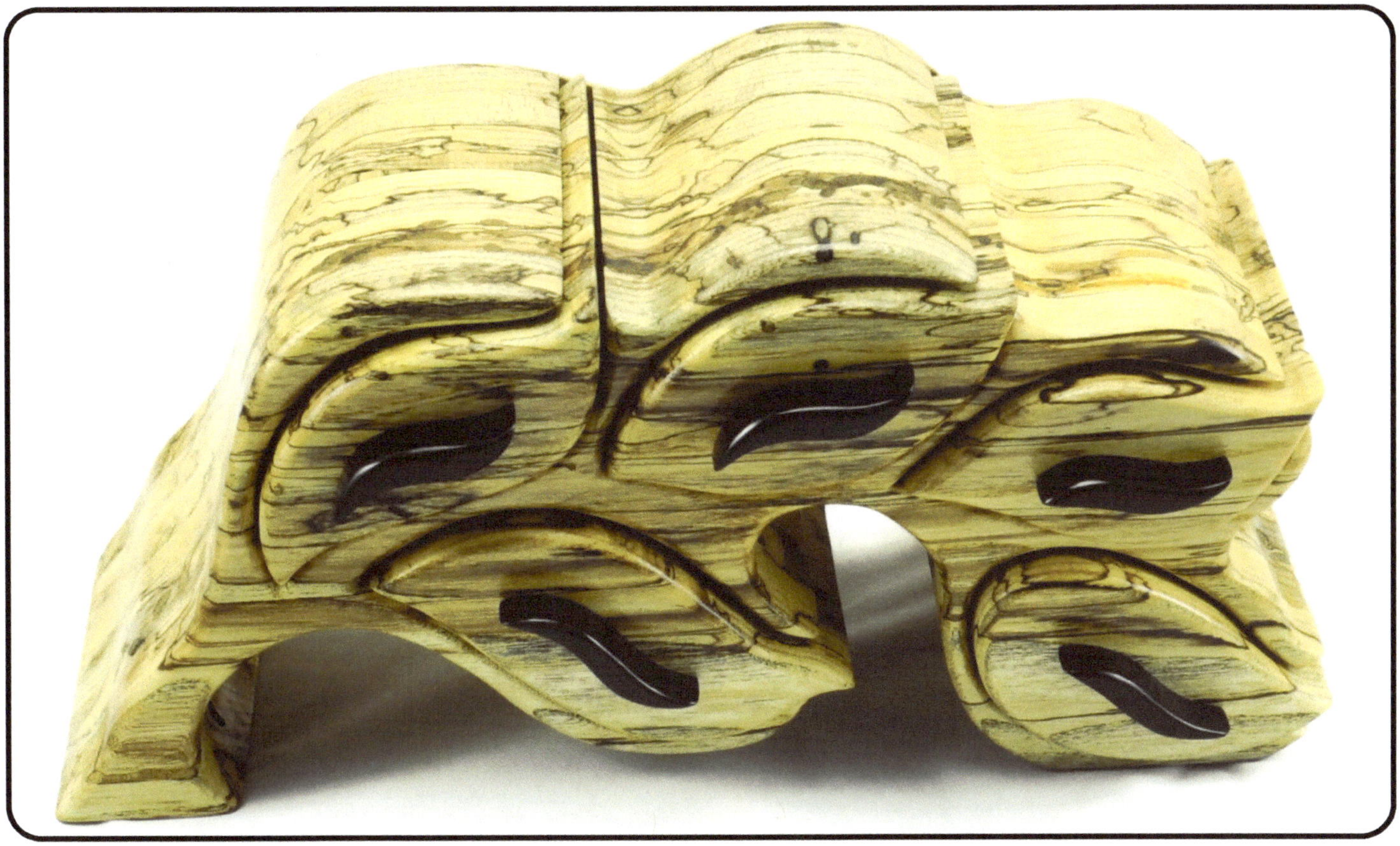

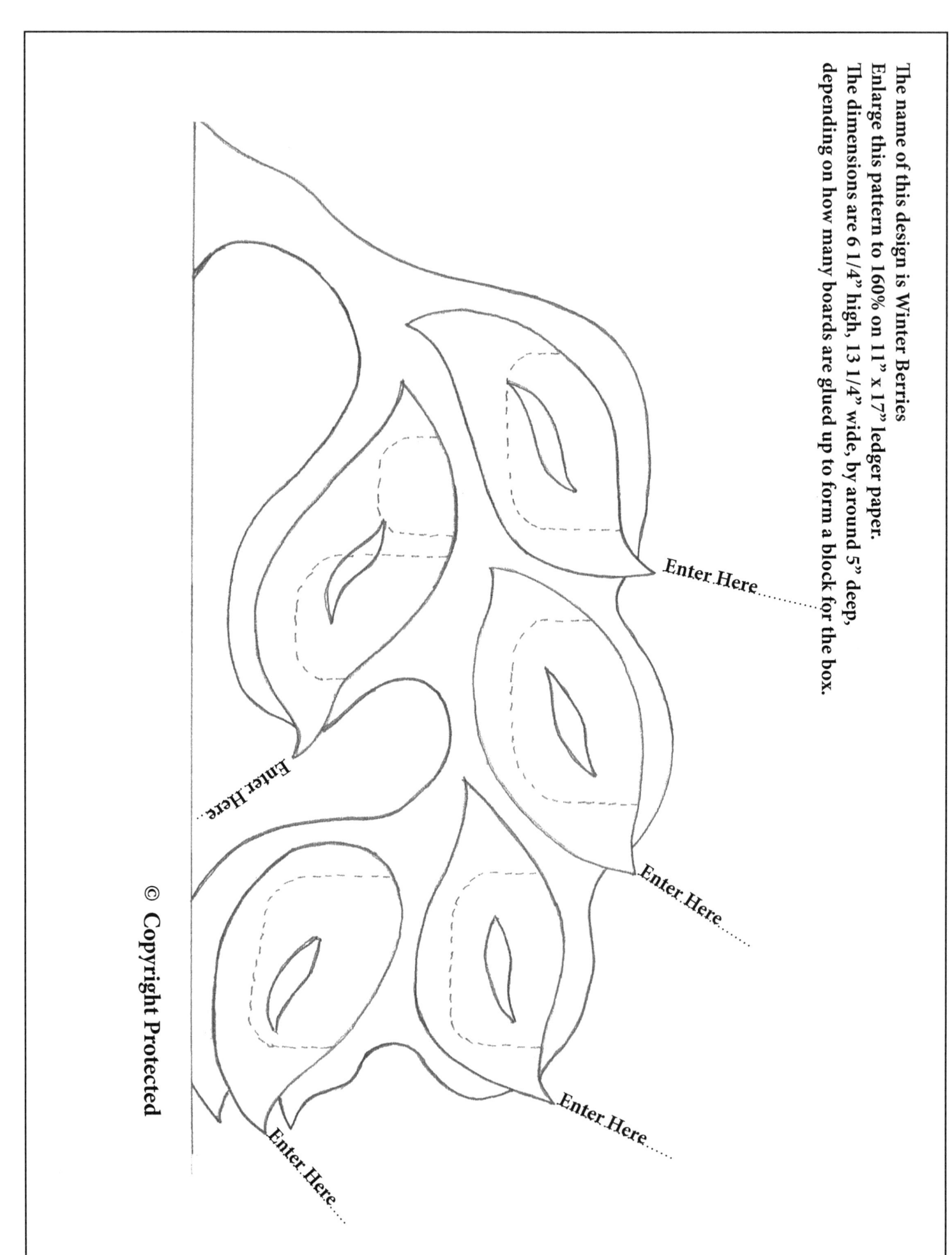

The name of this design is Winter Berries
Enlarge this pattern to 160% on 11" x 17" ledger paper.
The dimensions are 6 1/4" high, 13 1/4" wide, by around 5" deep, depending on how many boards are glued up to form a block for the box.

© Copyright Protected

Artistry In Woodworking

Skylarker

This box was handcrafted with Birdseye Maple and South American Purple Heart for the drawer pulls

The name of this design is Skylarker Enlarge this pattern to 130% on 8 1/2" x 14" legal paper. The dimensions are 5 1/4" high, 11 1/4" wide, by around 5" deep, depending on how many boards are glued up to form a block for the box.

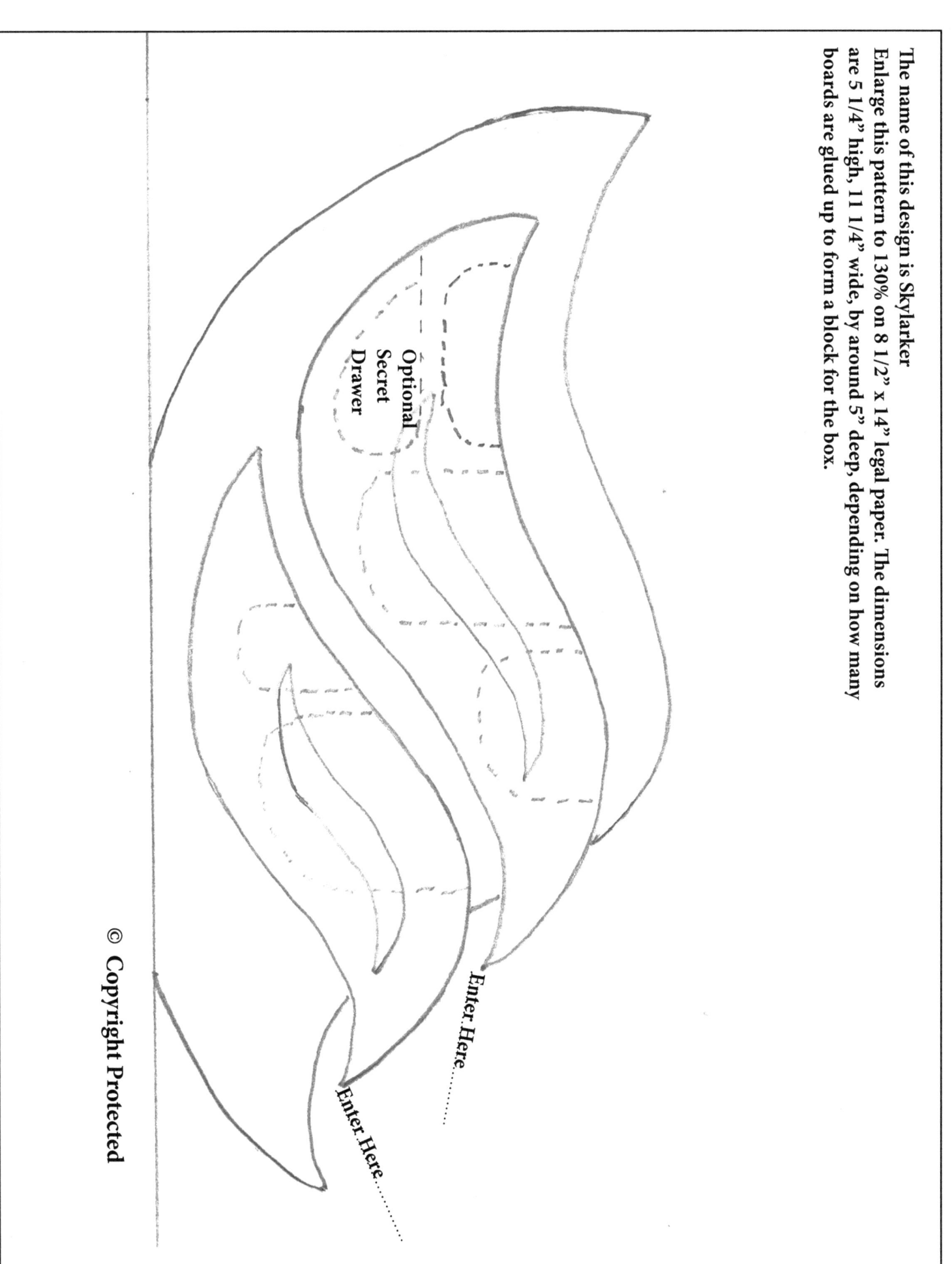

Optional Secret Drawer

Enter Here
Enter Here

© Copyright Protected

117

Artistry In Woodworking

Serengeti VI

This box was handcrafted with
Spalted Maple and African Ebony
for the drawer pulls

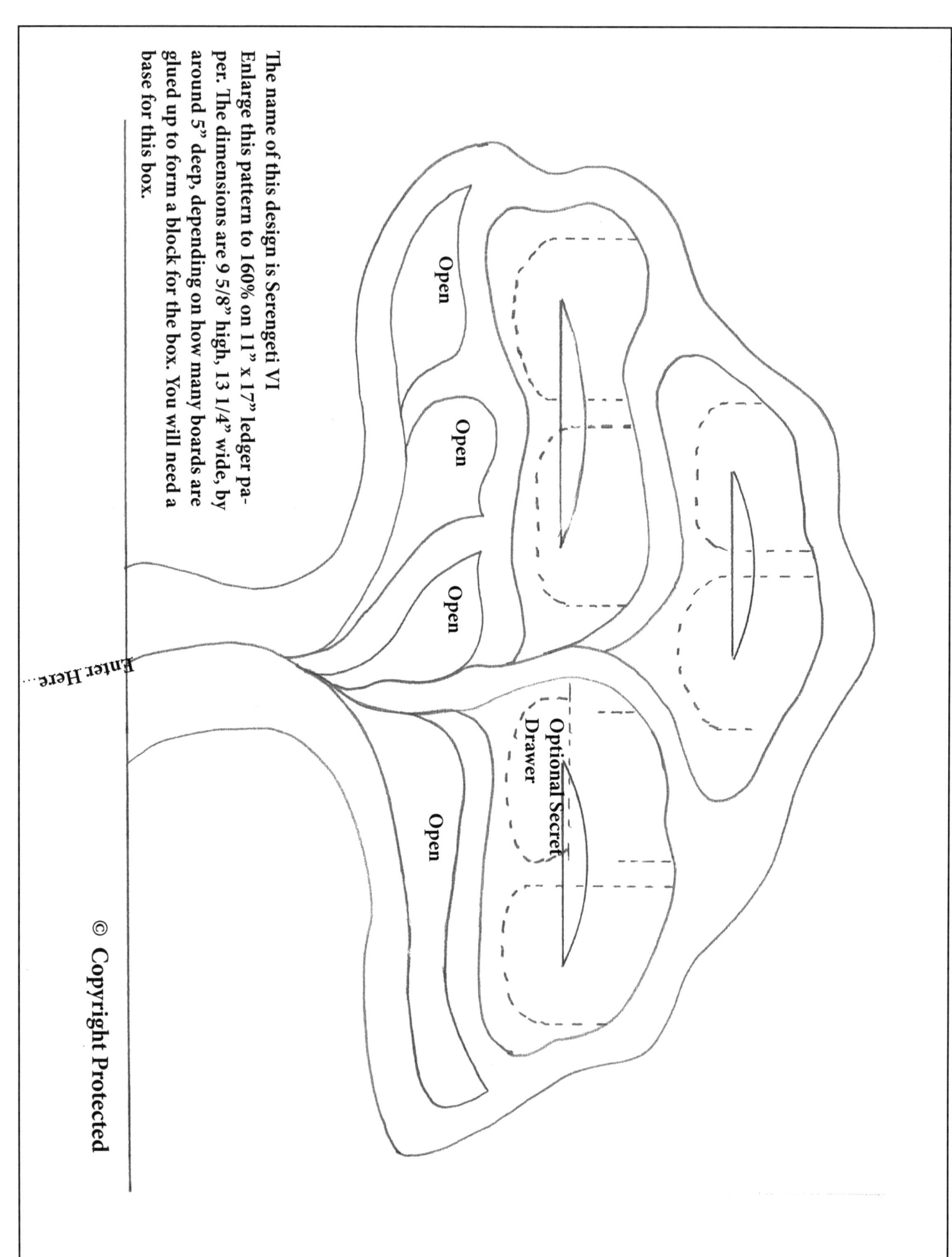

The name of this design is Serengeti VI. Enlarge this pattern to 160% on 11" x 17" ledger paper. The dimensions are 9 5/8" high, 13 1/4" wide, by around 5" deep, depending on how many boards are glued up to form a block for the box. You will need a base for this box.

© Copyright Protected

Artistry In Woodworking

Prancing Hemlock

This box was handcrafted with South American Yellow Heart and Buckeye Burl on the drawer fronts

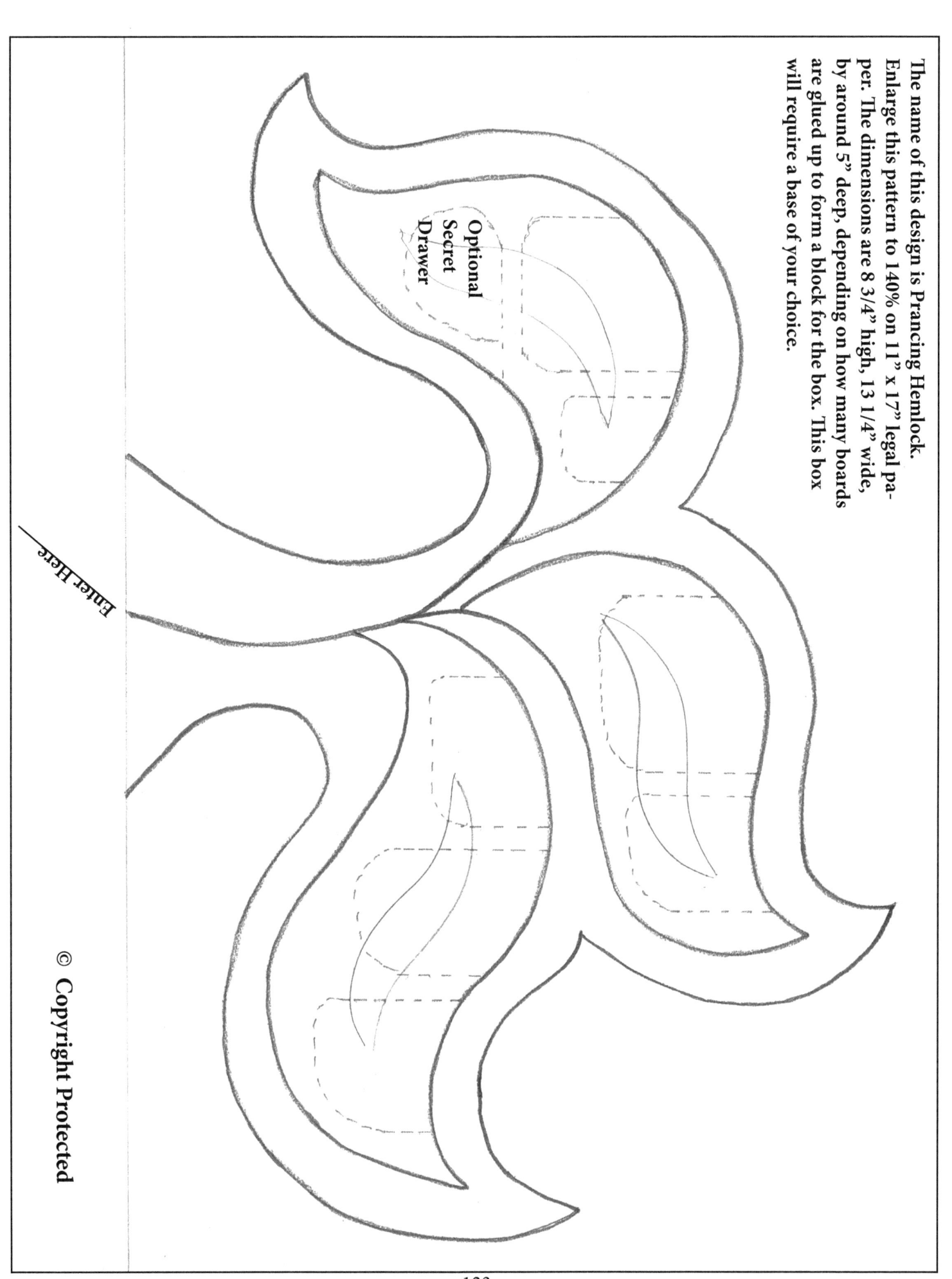

The name of this design is Prancing Hemlock. Enlarge this pattern to 140% on 11" x 17" legal paper. The dimensions are 8 3/4" high, 13 1/4" wide, by around 5" deep, depending on how many boards are glued up to form a block for the box. This box will require a base of your choice.

© Copyright Protected

Artistry In Woodworking

Free Spirits

This box was handcrafted with African Sapele and Buckeye Burl on the drawer fronts

The name of this design is Free Spirits. Enlarge this pattern to 140% on 8 1/2" x 14 legal paper. The dimensions are 6" high, 10 3/4" wide, by around 5" deep, depending on how many boards are glued up to form a block for the box.

Optional Secret Drawer

Enter Here
Enter Here
Enter Here

© Copyright Protected

Artistry In Woodworking

Reflections

This box was handcrafted with
Spalted Maple and African Ebony
for the drawer pulls

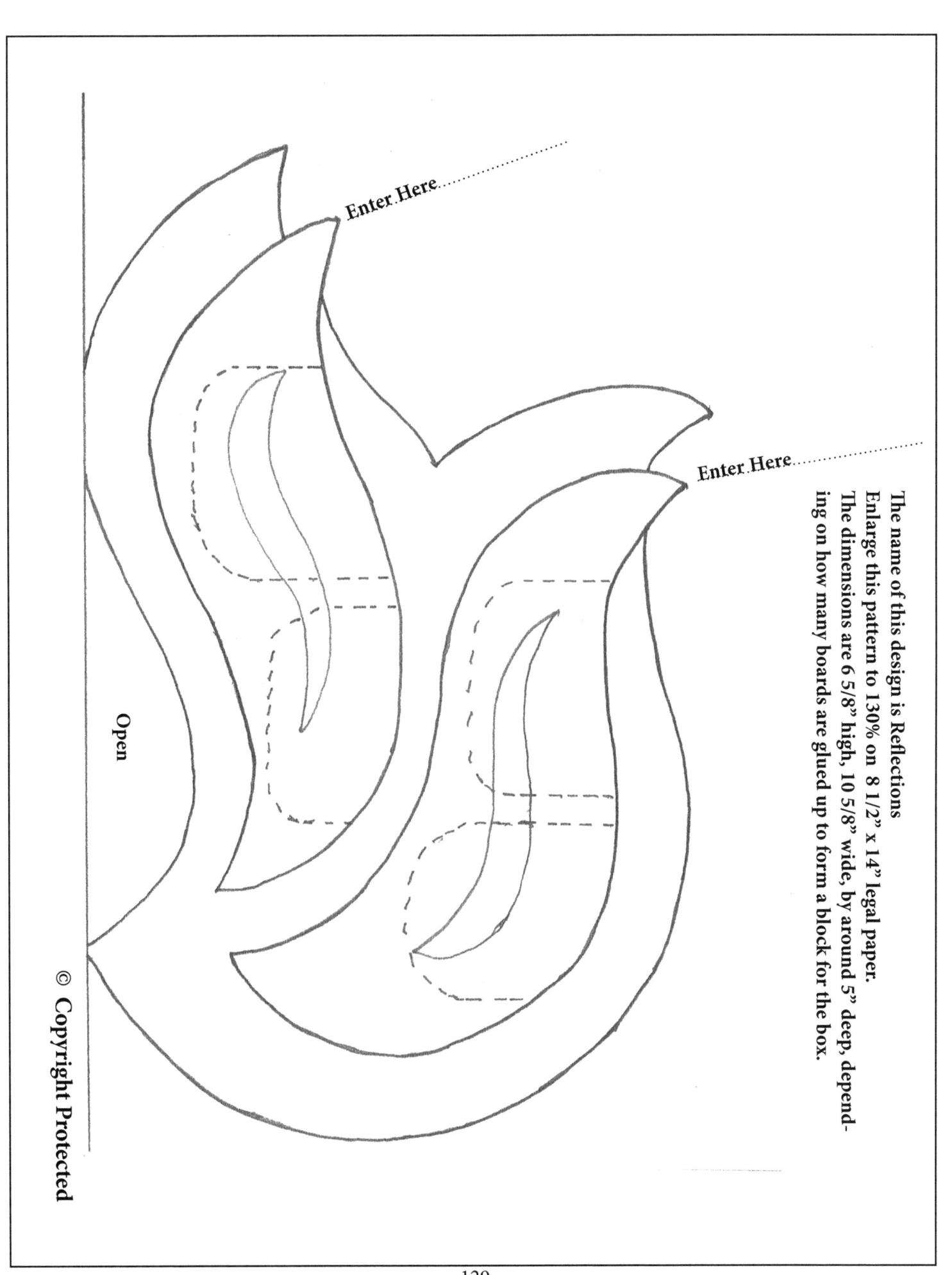

The name of this design is Reflections
Enlarge this pattern to 130% on 8 1/2" x 14" legal paper. The dimensions are 6 5/8" high, 10 5/8" wide, by around 5" deep, depending on how many boards are glued up to form a block for the box.

Notes:

Notes: